Each believer needs all the help we can get to respond with sensitivity, spiritual discernment and intercessory passion as we observe and relate to the long struggle between powers in the Middle East. This book helps.

—JACK W. HAYFORD, CHANCELLOR/PASTOR
THE KING'S COLLEGE AND SEMINARY
THE CHURCH ON THE WAY

There is a demonic strategy behind Islam's quest for world domination that all Christians must understand. First, Muslims are going after the "Saturday people" (the Jews). But then they will come for the "Sunday people" (the Christians). *Islam and the Jews* reveals the secret agenda that is not being told by the media.

When the Bush administration officials condemn Christian leaders for telling the truth about Islam, it is either because of ignorance or because they are trying to appease oil interests. I wish U.S. government officials would read *Islam and the Jews*.

—SID ROTH
PRESIDENT, MESSIANIC VISION

Dr. Gabriel's life transformation from devout Muslim to believing Christian is a powerful reminder of how love can indeed conquer hate and how faith can be a source of healing and reconciliation rather than a force of discord and destruction—a bridge that links Christians, Muslims and Jews together as children of Father Abraham.

Today, more than ever, we need to be informed about Islam—in *all* its manifestations—and recognize its forces for good as well as those that threaten to engulf us and destroy our Western values and civilization. This book is a bold eye-opener that will benefit all who read it. Dr. Gabriel's change of heart in becoming a Christian prompts him to bless the Jewish people rather than curse and hate them. He demonstrates in the clearest way the transforming power of his new-found Christian faith.

I was blessed to read how Dr. Gabriel's life became filled with love for the Jewish people when he had his "Road to Damascus" experience. I am confident that God will honor His Word and bless him accordingly, as He promised in Genesis 12:3, "I will bless those who bless [Israel]."

—RABBI YECHIEL ECKSTEIN, FOUNDER AND PRESIDENT
INTERNATIONAL FELLOWSHIP OF CHRISTIANS AND JEWS
CHICAGO AND JERUSALEM

ISLAM
and the
Jews

MARK A. GABRIEL, PH.D.

Charisma
HOUSE
A STRANG COMPANY

ISLAM AND THE JEWS by Mark A. Gabriel
Published by Charisma House
A Strang Company
600 Rinehart Road
Lake Mary, Florida 32746
www.charismahouse.com

Unless otherwise noted, all Scripture quotations are from the Holy Bible, New International Version. Copyright © 1973, 1978, 1984, International Bible Society. Used by permission.

Scripture quotations marked NKJV are from the New King James Version of the Bible. Copyright © 1979, 1980, 1982 by Thomas Nelson, Inc., publishers. Used by permission.

Unless otherwise noted, quotations from the Quran are from *The Noble Quran*, English Translation of the Meanings and Commentary published by King Fahd of Saudi Arabia in Medina, "The City of Light," Saudi Arabia in 1998. The translators were Dr. Muhammad Taqi-ud-Din Al-Hilali and Dr. Muhammad Muhsin Khan.

Quotations from the Quran marked ALI TRANSLATION are from *The Quran Translation*, 7th edition, by Abdullah Yusef Ali (Elmhurst, NY: Tahrike Tarsile Quran, Inc., 2001).

Cover design by Karen Gonsalves

Library of Congress Cataloging-in-Publication Data
    Gabriel, Mark A.
    Islam and the Jews / Mark A. Gabriel.
       p. cm.
    ISBN 0-88419-956-8 (Trade paper)
    1. Islam–Relations–Judaism. 2. Islam–Relations–Judaism. 3. Jews
    in the Koran. 4. Jewish-Arab relations–Religious aspects–Islam. 5.
    Islam–Controversial literature. I. Title.
    BP173.J8 G25 2003
    297.2'82–dc21
                                2002156464

05 06 07 08 09 — 9 8 7 6 5 4
Printed in the United States of America

Dedication

I dedicate this book to every Jewish man or
woman who is living in any part of our world,
and I take the opportunity to apologize for
the ungodly attitude I had during the first
thirty-four years of my life. I was blind, but
now I can see. I ask your forgiveness.

Whoever loves his brother lives in the light,
and there is nothing in him to make him stumble.
But whoever hates his brother is in the darkness
and walks around in the darkness;
he does not know where he is going,
because the darkness has blinded him.

—1 JOHN 2:10–11

Helps for
the Western Reader

MY GOAL IS TO MAKE THIS book as easy to understand as possible. In this brief introduction you will learn the definitions of a few key words about Islam and Judaism. In addition, I will explain some important information about quotations from the Quran. I will be quoting extensively from the Quran throughout this book because I want you to see that you are getting the facts, not opinions, about what Islam teaches.

KEY DEFINITIONS

ARABIC WORLD. The Arabic world has been defined as approximately twenty-two countries in the Middle East and North Africa where Arabic is spoken. (All of these countries have a Muslim majority.)

ARABS. The descendants of Abraham's son Ishmael. In modern times, the word *Arab* means people who speak Arabic and live in the Arabian Peninsula.

FUNDAMENTALIST MUSLIM GOVERNMENT: The only modern examples are Iran, Sudan and the former government of Afghanistan. The government is exclusively based on Islamic teachings.

GOSPELS (*Injeel* in Arabic). Matthew, Mark, Luke and John from the Christian New Testament. However, it is good to remember that only the Gospel of Matthew was available in Arabic during Muhammad's time.

HADITH. The teachings and actions of Muhammad, recorded by his followers (including some of his wives) and collected by Muslim scholars.

ISLAM. The religion based on the Quran and hadith.

ISLAMIC WORLD. The countries where most people practice Islam. There are about fifty-five Islamic countries in the world.

ISRAEL. The political state of Israel in the Middle East.

JUDAISM. The religion of the Jewish people, based on the wisdom and law contained in Jewish Scripture and other sacred literature and oral tradition.

MUSLIM. A person who practices Islam. May also be spelled *Moslem*.

NEW TESTAMENT. The twenty-seven books of the Christian New Testament.

OLD TESTAMENT. The thirty-nine books of the Old Testament in the Christian Bible.

PEOPLE OF THE BOOK. The phrase used in the Quran to refer to Jews and Christians.

PROPHET OF ISLAM. A way of referring to Muhammad, whose revelations formed the basis of Islam. He may also be referred to as the prophet Muhammad. This is the typical way Muhammad is referred to by people from the Middle East.

QURAN. The words of Allah revealed to Muhammad in seventh-century Arabia. The Quran is 114 chapters long—about the length of the Christian New Testament.

SECULAR MUSLIM NATIONS: Examples are Iraq, Jordan, Egypt, Syria, Lebanon and the Palestinian Authority. The leaders of these countries are Muslims, but their governments are not run exclusively according to Islamic law.

TORAH (*Taurat* in Arabic). When the Quran mentions the Taurat, it is referring to the first five books of the Jewish Scriptures written by Moses (Genesis, Exodus, Leviticus, Numbers, Deuteronomy).

QUOTATIONS FROM THE QURAN

The Quran was originally written in Arabic, and Muslims believe it can only properly be understood in Arabic. However, there are many English translations. When you are reading an English translation of the Quran, keep in mind that many times the Arabic meaning is translated accurately, but in some cases the true meaning is obscured by the translators. Most quotations from the Quran in this book are from the English translation known as *The Noble Quran* (translated by Dr. Muhammad Taqi-ud-Din Al-Hilali and Dr. Muhammad Muhsin Khan). You can purchase it at Amazon.com or other places on the Internet. This translation includes commentary in brackets, similar to the Amplified Bible in English. This makes it much easier to understand the intended meaning of the verses.

In some verses from the Quran you will notice the word *We* or *Our* in capital letters. The word will seem to be referring to Allah; however, Islam teaches that Allah is one God, which makes this term confusing. The explanation is that the usage of *We* is actually an Arabic language device to show the greatness and power of Allah. It doesn't mean plurality.

Finally, when I am citing a reference in the Quran, I will use the word *surah*. This means *chapter* in Arabic.

Contents

Prologue

WRITING ABOUT ISLAM AND THE JEWS is not just a research project for me. It was my life. The first thirty-four years of my life I treated others according to what the Quran and the prophet of Islam told me. I lived all those years for only one purpose: to serve Allah, the god of Islam, and to obey his prophet Muhammad. I became a scholar of Islam, memorizing the entire Quran and earning a doctorate degree in Islamic history and culture.

In Arabic we say, "It's no crime to grow up to look like your father." You will look like your father automatically. In the same way, it was natural for me to grow up with a great hatred toward the Jews because that is the true attitude of Islam. It was an honor for me to prove to the people around me and even to myself that I was really against the Jews. I took every opportunity to speak against them, to curse them, to spit on their gravestones. I did that because I was faithful to what I believed. I was like Saul of the New Testament, who was cursing and killing Christians and thinking that he was pleasing God this way.

I left Islam and accepted the Lord Jesus Christ as my Lord and Savior, but my attitude toward the Jews stayed the same for two years. Then God in His mercy knocked me off my feet and revealed Himself to me, just as He did to Paul.

The Great Surgeon, my Lord and Savior Jesus Christ, did powerful, heavenly surgery on my heart. I became a new creature with a new heart, new eyes and new brain. For the first time I recognized Jewish people as human beings, created by God and chosen by Him to carry His message to the entire world through the Jewish prophets from Isaac to the Messiah Jesus Christ.

My heart in this book is to help you see why Muslims have such a problem with Jewish people and what it will take to reconcile the two.

Introduction

ATER SEPTEMBER 11, 2001, I WROTE a book titled *Islam and Terrorism*. It gave the facts about how the teachings of Islam support terrorism.

In the book you are reading now, I turn your attention toward the place of the Jews in Islamic teaching. Again the situation in the world has pointed out the need for this book.

Wherever you see Islamic terrorism, you will hear of hatred toward the Jews and those who support Israel, in particular, the United States. Watch the news reports carefully the next time there is an attack. If a Muslim is interviewed, you will inevitably hear him complain that Israel and America are to blame. They are the real terrorists, he will argue. At the same time, Westerners watch in dismay and confusion as Israelis and Palestinian Muslims fight each other, taking an eye for an eye and a tooth for a tooth.

People are wondering, *Why can't Arab Muslims find a way to make peace with Israel?* In this book I will take you back to the Quran and Islamic history and show you the reasons that Muslims won't make peace.

MISLED BY MEDIA

What you are about to read is not just something I copied out of one book. I have pulled information from many different resources over years of scholarly research. My information about Islam is based on the Quran, the life of the prophet of Islam, Islamic history and personal experience. I have a doctorate degree in Islamic history and culture from Al-Azhar University. The information I present is much different from the information you get from Western writings.

The information in Western media is very misleading. A best-selling book about Islam used in high schools and colleges says:

> Muhammad never asked Jews or Christians to accept Islam unless they particularly wished to do so, because they had received perfectly valid revelations of their own.[1]
>
> The Quran continued to ... urge Muslims to respect the People of the Book.[2]
>
> Jews, like Christians, enjoyed full religious liberty in the Islamic empires.[3]

This book was also quoted frequently on the PBS special about the life of Muhammad.[4] Let me just say emphatically that these statements are not right, and in this book I will quote you the evidence from the Quran and hadith that will prove it. I am amazed at how people in the West misrepresent Islam in the name of tolerance.

MUSLIMS ARE NOT THE ENEMY

I am not trying to make Muslims look bad. But I am trying to present the true picture about Islam. People need to understand Islam in order to make sense of the world today. Secular Muslims need to understand what their religion really teaches. In fact, the only ones who won't be surprised by the contents of this book are committed Muslims. They know exactly what I am writing about.

Let me be clear that Muslims are not my enemies. Muslims are my family and my people that I left behind. I love them. What I am trying to do is to help them and others to see the truth about Islam. I am a free person, living in a free country, and I can ask the hard questions about Islam, but the Muslim people I left behind cannot question their beliefs.

I do not want to cause Westerns to hate Muslims, to be afraid of them or to treat them with contempt. Instead, I want the reader to be filled with anger toward the *teachings* of Islam itself.

I want you to see this very, very important distinction: *Islam* is the religion. It is Islam that creates all the bad attitudes and the problems. *Muslims* are people who are following Islam. Muslims are also the victims of Islam. In the entire world, they are the ones suffering the most from Islam. Because of Islam, they go through life trying to please Allah but never knowing whether they have succeeded. Because of Islam, they lose their lives fighting for Allah in hopes that this will get them into Paradise. Because of Islam they don't know how to forgive themselves or to forgive others.

Hate Islam, but love Muslims.

If you have Muslim friends, neighbors or acquaintances, be kind to them. They are probably nice people living in a peaceful way and not wanting to cause trouble for you or anybody else. Most likely they do not understand Islam very deeply, and they are practicing Islam in a nice way.

Do not treat them as your enemies. Do not use your knowledge of Islam to belittle them or to make fun of them. The best thing you can do is to enjoy their friendship. Enjoy their culture and accept opportunities to share your beliefs with them in a positive way.

Whenever you are discussing religion with someone else, keep a good attitude. You must be very sensitive because this is a serious subject, and every person wants to defend his faith. But we are all brothers and sisters in humanity—we are all searching for the truth. When we talk and listen without anger, God will guide us to truth.

WHAT YOU ARE ABOUT TO READ

Let me give you an overview of the organization of this book.

First, I give you a look into my life so that you can understand what I, and many Muslims like me, thought about the Jewish people. In order for you to appreciate how much I have changed, you need to see how deeply embedded my attitudes were. The change in my beliefs is something completely radical for a person raised in Islam.

Second, I need to introduce you to the basics of Islam. Without a solid understanding, you are going to struggle with the rest of the book. In particular, I want you to see that Muhammad had a tremendous change in attitude about halfway through his time as the leader of Islam. This created contradictions in the Quran. In one place he said to tolerate Jews; in another place he said to kill them. I will explain to you how the Quran told Muslims to handle these contradictions.

Third, I will give you a clear explanation, with direct quotes from the Quran, about the time when Muhammad was positive toward the Jews. He was trying to encourage them to convert to Islam. Appendix A explains the role of Abraham and Ishmael in Islam.

Fourth, I will show how Muhammad's attitude toward Jews changed and give you direct quotes from the Quran that document this. These teachings form the basis of Islamic beliefs about Jews today. You will also learn how Muhammad personally led brutal attacks against the Jews in his area. This is when Islam's unfinished battle against the Jews began, and it is still being fought today.

Fifth, you will see how the leaders of Islam who came after Muhammad followed his example. In particular, you can read the list of requirements that Jews had to follow in order to continue to practice their faith, including always wearing yellow to identify themselves as Jews. In a brief overview of the history between Jews and Muslims, you will find a chapter devoted to the Crusades. When people hear about Islamic history, many of them challenge me by saying, "I understand that Islam has a bloody history, but Christians also did terrible things during the Crusades. What's the difference?" I will give you the answer to this question.

Sixth, history will be brought to life in modern times. In particular, we'll look at the mind-set behind today's front lines of the unfinished battle—the fight between Israel and the Palestinians.

The final chapters of this book are for Christians. You will learn about the attitude of the church in the Middle East toward Israel. You will get a picture of the biblical way of reconciliation with the Jewish people. You will be thrilled by the testimonies of two former members of radical jihad groups. Finally, there is a detailed prayer guide for intercessors.

My prayer is that the Lord will use this book to help Muslims and Jews to find the way of reconciliation, to love one another and to forgive their historical hatred and animosity toward one another.

SECTION 1

MY NEW HEART
TOWARD THE JEWS

CHAPTER 1

First Impressions

I'LL NEVER FORGET THE MOMENT I heard them. I was playing in the street outside my house when I heard a sudden loud sound in the sky. It was the Israeli air force, flying like a dangerous bird over Egypt. The sky was literally full of planes. They were flying back and forth.

I started running into the house as fast as I could, but even before I got inside, the sky was yellow with explosions. I was so afraid that I didn't even look for my father or mother. All I could think to do was hide underneath my own bed to seek some way to escape. I was so panicked that I lost control of myself and soiled my pants. It was a horrible day.

The Israeli air force dropped bombs on my city, targeting a bridge and some buildings. Some people were killed, and many injured. After fifteen minutes, the sound of the airplanes was gone. People were running through the streets, looking for family and friends, asking what happened.

HUMILIATION

After six days, the Israeli military had destroyed the Egyptian military. Thousands of Egyptians were killed, and thousands were taken prisoners of war. The Israeli army took all of the Sinai Desert and marched across the Suez Canal. They were marching through Egypt, on their way to Cairo. At one point they were less than forty miles from the city.

The people in Cairo were shaking with fear over what might happen if the Israeli military took over Cairo. Would they have the same fate as the Palestinians? We expected death in an ocean of blood.

The Israeli air force terrified people the most. The Egyptian air force was destroyed after the first day. There were no Egyptian planes to go up and defend the sky.

This was my experience of the Six-Day War in 1967. I was ten years old.

ANGER AND FEAR

On the third or fourth day of the war, I had a dream.

In my dream, my father took a little fishing boat and went to catch fish in the Nile River. He was using a big net. He had it spread out between the boat and the shore with weights to keep one side on the bottom.

There weren't any Jewish people in Egypt at that time, but in my dream there were Jewish people who would tie up their cows next to the Nile and let them spend the day there. One of the cows got loose, got into the water and destroyed my father's net.

My father saw that the cow destroyed the net, and he went to the Jewish man and said, "Why did you let your cow do that?" They started arguing. Some other Jews came to support this man in his argument with my father. Then all of them took my father, beat him and left him on the edge of the bank of the Nile.

When the Jewish people saw my family members running to rescue my father, they left their cows, jumped in my father's boat and tried to get away on the river.

One of the people from my clan found me in the fields around my home and asked, "What are you doing here?"

"I'm studying," I replied.

He said, "Your father has died. The Jewish people have killed him."

In my dream I ran quickly to my house, but I didn't find anyone home. I rushed over to the cabinet where my father always put his gun. The key wasn't there, so I kicked open the cabinet door, grabbed a gun and ran to the riverbank.

When I arrived at the river, I saw the Jewish people in my father's boat. I stood on the bank of the river and aimed at them with the gun. One after another, I shot them as they tried to flee in the boat. In my dream it was like shooting birds. One by one they fell out of the boat into the water.

Can you see how deep my fear and anger were? Can you imagine what it would take to change my heart?

The Six-Day War was the final brick that completed the wall of hatred in my heart against the Jews. But this wall wasn't built in one day (or a week). The foundation was laid when I was very young, through a book called the Quran.

CHAPTER 2

Memorizing
the Quran

WHEN I WAS A LITTLE CHILD, one of the highlights of the week was when the Quran reciter visited our house. A Quran reciter is a man who has memorized the Quran and recites it in people's homes or for special occasions. The Muslims in my area believed his reciting would drive away evil spirits, bring the blessing of Allah and protect the house from thieves.

The Quran reciter came to our house twice a week. As a child, I remember the black glasses he wore and the nice sound of his voice. My grandmother, my mother and I always listened to him together. My grandmother was very old, she had a lame foot, and she was very weak. When the sheikh* came, she would relax on the sofa and put a pillow behind her back to get comfortable. She seemed like a little girl at these times, enjoying nice stories from her teacher.

Usually the sheikh recited for one hour. Afterward my mother gave him a cup of coffee to help to take away the headache that he usually had after reciting the Quran. While he drank coffee, he told us stories about the prophet Muhammad and his early friends and their relationship with idol worshipers, Arabs, Jews and Christians in the area. These stories were often about Muhammad's

---

* A title of honor for a Muslim leader

battles with the Jewish people in Arabia.

To help the Western reader picture this scene, it was kind of like Christian and Jewish children listening to the stories from the Bible, such as Joshua fighting the battle of Jericho or David conquering Goliath. The difference was that Muhammad's enemy was still our enemy, and that enemy was now living in the state of Israel right next to Egypt.

My mother was very proud of the way the prophet Muhammad fought to protect his revelation from being destroyed by idol worshipers, Jews and Christians. But she was also unsettled when she heard how the prophet Muhammad took the women and children as slaves and gave them to his military soldiers or sold them in the slave market.

One day I asked her about that. She told me, "I was expecting the prophet to be more merciful with the women and children. I believe he had the right to defend his revelation by fighting and killing the people who tried to harm him and his revelation. But the women and children—they didn't sin; they didn't do anything against him . . . " My mother had such a tender heart.

The Quran reciter always presented Jewish people in an evil way. He told us, "They are the source of all evil. They are unfaithful. They aren't trustworthy. They hate Islam and hate the prophet of Islam, and they persecuted him and his early friends. They were always trying to find an opportunity to kill the prophet of Islam and to destroy his revelations."

MONKEYS AND PIGS

Every time he came to our house, the sheikh had something new to tell us. One day he recited from Surah 5, and I heard something that really piqued my curiosity. It was verse 60, which told the horrible fate of "those (Jews) who incurred the Curse of Allah and His Wrath, and those of whom (some) He transformed into monkeys and swine."

I had to know more about that subject. I asked the sheikh, "Is it really true that Allah turned a group of Jewish people into monkeys and pigs?" I was thinking about the pigs that I saw in the yards of the Christians in our area. I also thought about the monkeys in the zoo and how I liked to feed them bananas and peanuts from Sudan.

He said, "Yes, my son, you have heard the Quran, which I have just recited to you, and what it was talking about. Allah told us this story in the Quran, and Allah never lies to us, my son. But the people who were cursed and transformed into monkeys and pigs, these were the Jewish people because they were rebellious toward Allah and persecuted and killed his prophets (Surah 5:70). This is why Allah cursed them and transformed them into monkeys and pigs."

This story was one of many I heard from the sheikh, and they planted a horrible seed of hatred in my heart day after day against the Jewish people.

Soon I would do more than just sit and listen to stories. My family decided that I would have the honor of becoming a reciter myself—and I began to memorize the Quran.

MEMORIZING THE QURAN

Many people in the West can hardly imagine that a child could memorize the Quran. But for people from the Middle East, this is something that is easily understood.

When I was growing up, the way of life for a child in Egypt was much different from that for a child in the West. When I was a child, I never went to a movie. There were no clubs or special groups for children. We had no library where we could go and get children's books. Until recently, there was no TV programming for children. In my time, we didn't even have a television in our home.

Of course, I played with my friends and did things with my family. But I had a lot of free time to devote to the Quran.

STARTING YOUNG

When I was very young, before I could read, my uncle would help me memorize some short chapters from the Quran. He would read the verses to me, and I would repeat them until I could say them on my own. Later I attended Al-Azhar primary institute. At this school, all of us were striving to memorize the Quran, which is about the length of the New Testament. I had about forty-five students in my class.

From age six to twelve, I had to memorize about two pages a day. I had to finish memorizing those two pages before the sun came up in the morning. Every day in school I recited to my teacher what I had memorized the day before.

A student who was unable to recite the new passage was usually beaten. For beating, the student was required to sit in a chair and remove his shoes and socks. One of the instructor's assistants put a belt around the student's ankles and secured them tightly together. Then he lifted the student's legs by the ankle until they were straight out, perpendicular to his body. The instructor would then beat the student on the bottom of his feet with a thick palm frond stem, freshly cut and green. It hurt—and I did everything I could to avoid it.

I was also motivated in a positive way by a desire to please my family. They were very proud of my studies.

EARLY MORNING STUDY

Most mornings I would go with my father and uncle to the morning prayers at the mosque, which started at 3:30 A.M. and finished at 4:30 A.M. After the prayers, my father and uncle usually went home to sleep two more hours before getting up for work. I usually stayed in the mosque with my copy of the Quran. Before I started memorizing the new verses, I tested myself on the passages I memorized on the two previous days. After I made sure my memorization was OK, I started the new material. I read the first verse of the passage. Then I closed my Quran and repeated the verse as I walked from corner to corner to corner of the mosque. When I finished the first verse, I opened my Quran and read the second verse. I continued this way until my memorizing was done.

I was very careful to retain what I had learned, so I spent two or three days a month in review. If you asked me about something I had memorized months earlier, it was there in my mind. At the end of the year, I took an oral exam covering all I memorized during the year. During the exam, two teachers would take turns asking questions. Sometimes they would ask me to recite verses from certain chapters. At other times, they would begin reciting a verse and ask me to name the surah (chapter) and continue reciting in the same place.

This was my routine all through elementary school. My cousin, who memorized the Quran before me, was my inspiration. Even though he went to university to study dentistry, he never stopped reciting the Quran. After I had finished memorizing the Quran (at age twelve), I started studying the commentary to the Quran so that I could understand what I had memorized.

LIVING BY THE QURAN

My study of the Quran went along perfectly with what was happening in my world because the Quran is full of teaching about the danger of Jews and how much trouble they caused the prophets. (Sections 2–4 of this book will tell you this information in detail.) As Muslims we felt that this was the time to defend our land and our faith—just as Muhammad did.

CHAPTER 3

My Missing Brother

WHEN I WAS ABOUT TEN YEARS old, Egypt was preparing for war with Israel. President Nasser had launched a massive propaganda campaign, with the media filling our ears about the threat of Israel at our border. Schools taught us that the Jews were our historical enemies who stole land away from the Palestinian Muslims. They said that it was our duty as Muslims to cut this cancer from our land and remove it.

In the summertime when it was hot, people sat outside of their homes eating nuts, drinking tea and talking about Israel. A favorite topic was the two past wars with Israel—1948 and 1956. They rehearsed the history between Islam and the Jews—how they tried to kill Muhammad, how much the Jews hate Muslims and how there is no way for Muslims to accept these people.

I often heard a particular story about Israel taking over one of the villages in Palestine. In Egypt, people said that the Israeli military surrounded the village, locked all the doors so no one could get away and then bombed the houses. They also claimed that Israeli soldiers would slice open pregnant women, kill the babies and then kill the women.

Now I know those stories were fabricated, but at the time we all accepted them as fact.

The First Nightmares

I had so internalized what was going on that I started having dreams about the leader of the Israeli military, Moshe Dayan. I had never seen a Jewish person face to face in my life, but I had seen this man's picture in the newspaper. He always wore a black patch over one eye. Many children had nightmares of Moshe Dayan appearing in their dreams as a one-eyed man with a horrible face.

One day, just a couple of months before the Six-Day War, I was taking an afternoon nap when I had a dream.

In my dream I saw one of the social clubs in my area where people would get coffee or tea and sit on the grass and just talk and play games. I went up to the entrance and went inside the door. There were no people. But I found Moshe Dayan. He was sitting on a small rock, and there was the body of an Egyptian person in front of him. Moshe Dayan had a butcher knife in his hand, and he was cutting the body into pieces.

In my dream I jumped up and fell backward onto the ground. A neighbor I knew helped me stand up, and I started running away. At that moment I woke up, and I recognized that I was at home. But I was sure that Moshe Dayan was in my house with a big knife and that he was going to cut me up just as he cut up the body in my dream.

I ran out into the street, crying and shouting. I ignored everyone around me and kept running toward the end of the street where there was an irrigation canal. I was going to jump in because I was so sure that Moshe Dayan was after me.

My father and brothers were running down the street after me, trying to catch up to me. My favorite brother reached me first and tackled me to the ground at the bank of the canal. Everyone took me back to our house where I sat with my mother while my father, brothers, uncle and neighbors surrounded us.

My brother said, "What happened? What happened?" So I told them, and they were shocked. My father said, "There is no Moshe Dayan at home. There is no one at home." They were afraid I was being bothered by a devil, so my uncle recited the last chapter of the Quran over me.

Just a few weeks later, four of my brothers, including my favorite, left to be a part of the Egyptian army that was amassing in the Sinai Desert in preparation to attack Israel. Each time a brother left the house to take the train, I carried one of his bags, walked with him to the train station and waited until the train came.

I was very afraid about what Israel might do to my country—and to my brothers. Soon my fears would no longer be confined to my dreams.

Israel struck first. The Israeli air force came and bombed us. As Egypt's defeat became quickly evident, my family and I could think of only one thing—my four brothers in the military. Three of my brothers returned home after about two months. But my favorite brother—the one who stopped me from jumping into the canal—wasn't heard from. The Egyptian military listed him as missing in action. Eight months passed with no news.

During this time, I cried in my sleep every night. My mother cried so much that she ran out of tears. All the time, she cried. When she cooked food, she cried. When she ate, she cried. Sometimes she cried without tears. At times, we were afraid that she was going crazy.

What was happening confirmed everything we had heard in the Quran. We said in my family, "Allah never lies. He told us through the Quran that we would never have peace with the Jews until Resurrection Day."

I missed my brother terribly. He was the one who taught me to swim in the Nile River when I was four years old. Now I would go to the Nile and just sit and stare at the spot where he would lay his clothes on the riverbank when we swam.[1]

I had a dream about this brother. In my dream he came to me and said, "What are you doing here?"

I said, "I'm studying."

He told me, "It's enough studying. Go enlist! Who is going to defend our country? Who is going to defend our religion?"

A SMALL VICTORY

One day my mother happened to meet the postman as he was coming to our house. He said, "You have a letter," and handed it to her.

My mother couldn't read, so she asked, "Letter from whom?"

"It is from the government," he said. My mother was worried. She thought the letter might be saying that we had to pay more taxes or something like that. She wasn't thinking it had anything to do with my brother.

She tucked the letter in her blouse, went into the house to her bedroom and put the letter under her pillow because there was no one to read it to her. My brothers and I were at school, and my father was at work. My sister was at home, but she wasn't taught to read either.

Around noontime, my mother noticed my uncle across the street, so she brought the letter to him. My uncle opened it, read quickly and announced, "It is from the government...and it says your son is alive!" My mother cried and cried and cried. My uncle shouted, "Thanks to Allah— he is alive!"

My aunt, my sister and other women from the neighborhood came to be with my mother. They went in the house, turned on some Egyptian music and danced together with happiness.

When the men got home, they celebrated in their own way. My father got out his rifle, stood in front of the house and shot into the air over and over again. My oldest brother did the same with his handgun. My uncle was also shooting from the roof of his house.[2]

All the neighbors came over to see what was going on. They knew it was either a big fight or a big celebration. My father prepared a big meal for everyone, and we all drank sharbat (a sweet, nonalcoholic punch). People came by our house for days to congratulate us.

My brother's military group had surrendered to Israel in the Sinai Desert, and they were taken prisoner. At first the prisoners had been allowed no communication while in Israel, but after six months they were permitted to send a letter. It took two more months for us to hear from the Egyptian government that my brother was alive.

Two months later my brother came home, clean shaven, wearing a nice military uniform and very happy to see his family.

MY NUMBER ONE ENEMY

What had life taught me by the age of ten? I knew for sure that the Jews were my number one enemy. They tried to kill my prophet, they took my brother prisoner, and their planes bombed my town. I believed every problem in the world was caused by the Jews. I hated anything that was in any way remotely connected to something Jewish.

CHAPTER 4

Speaking Out Against
My Enemy

As I grew up, nothing in my life ever challenged my opinion against the Jews. My opinion was just reinforced again and again. The only change was that as an adult, I had ways to express what I thought.

Here are some glimpses of my life to help you see my attitude.

THE JEWISH CEMETERY

After earning my bachelor's degree, I had to go into mandatory military service for a year. I was assigned to a missile base and worked in an underground bunker that housed the operation room. Ironically, my job was to watch for enemy airplanes, particularly from Israel. I also led the soldiers in prayers at the mosque on base. There were about one hundred fifty people there.

During that time, when I visited home on my days off, I had to take a bus to the Basatin neighborhood of South Cairo. From there I had a short walk to get a different bus or subway to go to my village. On the way I would pass a Jewish cemetery, where Jews had been buried one or two hundred years earlier. I often walked through the cemetery and looked at the tombstones. When I found one with a Star of David or writing in Hebrew, I would spit at it, or sometimes urinate on it, and curse: "O most evil people, you are an evil generation from an evil generation. I thank Allah that you do not exist here [in Egypt] anymore."

According to Islamic teaching, after death a person stays in the grave until judgment day. For Muslims, the grave is a place of peace. But for evil people, the grave holds painful punishment. So I imagined that every Jewish grave I walked over had a fire burning the person inside. I imagined them crying for help.

At these times, I felt satisfaction and peace in my heart because the Quran and the prophet Muhammad told me that evil people (such as my enemy the Jews) were punished in the grave. I never imagined that the prophet Muhammad or the Quran would lie to me, so I was 100 percent sure the Jewish people were burning in their graves. In that cemetery full of Jews, I felt as if I were walking above a lake of fire.

I felt it was my duty to visit the cemetery and curse the Jews, because the Quran says that Allah and Allah's people will curse the Jews until the judgment day (Surah 2:159). I was doing my part.

Many times I talked about this in my sermons at the mosque. I would command the people, "When you walk close to that cemetery, you must give Allah the joy of cursing the children of pigs and monkeys."

THE JEWISH NEIGHBORHOOD

After my military service, I started working on my master's and doctorate degrees at Al-Azhar University. I lived at my parent's home and took a bus to a square in Cairo. From there I liked to walk to the school because the road went through a beautiful neighborhood with houses and shops. This was the area of the city where Jews had once lived before they went to live in the new state of Israel. There were Muslims living in these houses now, but because Jews once occupied the houses, I would spit at the houses and curse at them. I would say, "Praise be to Allah that the Jews are gone. Praise be to Muhammad for driving them out." I did this on my walk to the university every day of the week.

SERMON MATERIAL

When I was a student, I served as an imam at a mosque outside of Cairo for a while. (This is similar to serving as a pastor or a rabbi.) After Friday prayers, I would deliver the sermon. Sometimes my entire sermon would be about Jews. The people at the mosque really enjoyed these sermons. Whenever I quoted verses from the Quran about the Jews, I would say, "All the children of the monkeys and the pigs, the most evil people in the world, where will you run away from the punishment of Allah?" Then the people would shout back *"Allah o akbar! Allah o akbar!"* (Allah is great! Allah is great!)

I loved to use the insulting text from Surah 62:5:

> The likeness of those who were entrusted with the (obligation of the) Taurât (Torah) (i.e. to obey its commandments and to practise its laws), but who subsequently failed in those (obligations), is as the likeness of a donkey which carries huge burdens of books (but understands nothing from them).

I explained to the people:

> The Jews were given the Torah, the most powerful book, and they were entrusted to carry it, but later Allah found them like donkeys, carrying the books, but not able to understand them and use them for benefit. They are just stupid animals.

I exalted Muhammad's harsh dealings with the Jews. I taught:

The Jewish people thought Muhammad would be like the other prophets sent to them. They would reject, persecute and kill him. But Muhammad was totally different from the prophets who came before him. Muhammad was the last messenger. He knew how to deal with the Jews and how to discipline them and how to give them a lesson that they never got from any prophet before him.

When I think back to how I used to talk, I am sorry that those words ever came out of my mouth. I was just a stupid person then. I was blind, but now I see.

ATTITUDE LINGERING

Even after I became a Christian, my Muslim attitude about the Jews stayed with me. If I passed a Jewish man on the street, it was to me just like seeing dirt walking in the street.

After I became a Christian, I left Egypt and went to live in Johannesburg, South Africa, I didn't have any personal encounters with Jews until one day in the spring of 1996. At the First National Bank in Johannesburg, I got in line to get some money from the ATM machine. The person behind me was a Jewish man wearing a yarmulke on his head. Because of my old Muslim attitudes, his presence made me very uncomfortable. I tried my best not to get too close to him so that he wouldn't accidentally brush up against me. I still thought of Jews as dirty and impure. I was always moving, turning my face away, trying to make sure I didn't look directly at his face.

When it was my turn at the machine, I had trouble because of my weak English. So I left the machine and went up the steps to the inside of the bank. One of the people who worked at the bank said, "OK, I'll come and help you."

So he came back with me, and we saw that the Jewish

person had started to use the machine. I still had the Muslim mentality, so I said in a rude way, "Excuse me. We are using this machine now. I was standing in front of you."

The Jewish man started to reply, but I interrupted him and spoke in a very ugly way to him. "You are dirt. You are not more than dirt. OK? Don't talk too much to me…" Really—I was very bad to him. I am embarrassed even to talk about how I acted.

He just stared at me as if I were crazy. I said, "Look—I'm an Egyptian. I'm from Egypt. You are a Jew. You understand [the relationship between us]."

There were other people in the line, and they just stared at me. *Where did this guy come from?* The Jewish man was shocked that I treated him like that. I'm sure he was thinking, *Who is this stupid man?*

The people in the line asked, "Sir, sir, why are you doing this? You tried to use the machine, and you left. The bank is not just for you. It is for everybody here."

The bank worker also said to me, "Just wait and let this man [the Jewish man] finish."

But the Jewish man stepped back and said, "Go ahead." He looked at the bank worker and said, "Sir, just help him." This man pitied me. He just wanted me to finish my transaction and go away.

DISCOVERING MY GUILT

Because I had already become a Christian by that time, I went to my Christian mentors, a husband and wife, and told them what had happened. My friend was Lebanese, and because Lebanon had been invaded by the Israeli military, I thought my friend would be happy to hear how I treated the Jewish man. I also wanted him to explain to me why the people at the bank seemed to take the side of the Jewish man.

21

I was still mixed up in my thinking about the Bible and the Quran. The Quran told me that the Jews were the killers of the prophets. The Bible also told me that the Jews killed Jesus. I hadn't yet recognized that the Jews are still God's chosen people despite the mistakes they have made.

My friends were very surprised by my attitude. The man said angrily, "Those Arab people poisoned your brain and your life when you were in Egypt. Those people have no compassion for others."

I felt very guilty after he talked to me. His wife showed me the new way of living. She told me to read a scripture in the Bible—John 3:16. "Jesus came for Jews, Muslims, Hindus, all the people," she told me. "If you are really a Christian, you must show your love to all these people." This was a completely new thought to me.

She gave me another verse in Ephesians:

> Put off, concerning your former conduct, the old man which grows corrupt according to the deceitful lusts, and be renewed in the spirit of your mind, and that you put on the new man which was created according to God, in true righteousness and holiness.
> —EPHESIANS 4:22–24, NKJV

She said, "Just read these scriptures and pray about it, and see what God will show you."

The next morning I told her, "These scriptures show me that I am guilty." This was the beginning, but I had a long way to go. I needed more to recognize my guilt. I needed power greater than myself to change me on the inside.

CHAPTER 5

How My Heart Changed

I FACED A DEFINING MOMENT WHEN I was at a Christian training center in Cape Town, South Africa. To make a long story short, they were ready to kick me out.

I was supposed to stay on the campus for three months in a Youth With A Mission (YWAM) discipleship training school. The other students and I were to spend time in Bible study, prayer, chores and relationship building. Instead I was argumentative, refused to work, refused to eat any of the pork they served in the cafeteria* and walked out on some speakers.

There was an American lady there, and I wouldn't even speak to her because, from my point of view, Americans deserved the same treatment as Jews because the U.S. supports Israel.

I knew that I needed to find a way to subdue the old man inside of me. I just didn't know how to do it. My own will power was too weak. Every day I went to the beach, which was just a few blocks from the base. I would walk by the ocean, crying out to God to help me change my attitude, my character and the way I treated other people. I could feel God's presence softening my heart at these times, and I knew He had to be the one to help me. No person could do it.

---

* The Quran prohibits Muslims from eating pork.

But my behavior really wasn't improving. One morning a base leader finally told me to change my ways or pack my suitcases. I knew my guilt, and I felt really broken inside.

I was alone in my room, crying from deep inside, and I felt that I needed to go to the beach and pray. I walked and prayed and finally just lay down in the sand, crying and crying. I fell asleep and began to dream.

I saw a person walking on the sea toward me. He was wearing a shiny white robe, and His face was golden. There was light all around Him. I noticed a Jewish prayer shawl around His neck.

He had bare feet, and I saw the water splashing around His feet as He walked. He came to me on the beach and then sat behind me. He put both hands on my shoulders and then spoke into my left ear. He said, "Today everything will be OK. I know you have been crying all the time because you want to change. First, I want you to humble yourself. Stop judging others. Accept anything they give you to eat in your school. Be faithful to Me, and be kind to everyone."

Then He wiped the tears from my face and hugged me with His right arm. He gently put His hand on my head and ruffled my hair (the kind of thing you would do a child), and then He left.

At that moment, a wave came and soaked me to the waist, and I woke up. I stared out to the sea and saw no one.

This was a clear message to me. God touched my heart and my brain. I felt the change. I felt the unseen power take the pain and anger away. I felt that my heart, memory and brain had been washed.

I was so excited that I ran back to the base. First, I went to find the American lady. She was in her room, sitting on her bed with a Bible on her lap. I could see by the tears on her face that she was crying. When she saw me, she set the Bible to the side and stood up. She said, "The Lord told me that today is the day of deliverance for you. I want you to know that I never stopped praying for you during this month. I asked the Lord to help you in the struggle."

I told her, "Please forgive me for the way I treated you. I saw the Lord today on the beach, and He changed my heart."

The next test was lunch. I could smell the sausage cooking, and it really turned my stomach. But I said to myself, "If I do not eat pork today, I am not a child of God." And I did it. You cannot believe the sensation it caused in the cafeteria when they saw me eating pork.

SEEK AND YOU WILL FIND

This was the turning point in my Christian life. I am not saying that every person needs to have a dream to get the strength to please God. But that is what I needed, and that is what the Lord Jesus did for me.

Jesus said, "Here I am! I stand at the door and knock. If anyone hears my voice and opens the door, I will come in and eat with him, and he with me" (Rev. 3:20). This verse was written to Christians. To me it says that Jesus will not force Himself into anyone's life. But if you invite Him to come in, He will.

For all that time I had been inviting Him, searching for truth and crying out to Him, so He answered me. The Bible says, "You will seek me and find me when you seek me with all your heart" (Jer. 29:13; see also Proverbs 8:17 and Matthew 7:8).

INVITATION TO A JEWISH BIBLE STUDY

I wasn't a perfect person after that day, but I was able to meet new challenges in a much better way. I was a changed person, and everyone around me could see that. I finished the program at Youth With A Mission.

After students finish training with YWAM, they must spend two months working on a mission project of their choice. YWAM arranged for me to do outreach with a missionary couple in Cape Town who were working in the Muslim community. They befriended Muslims and spent time talking with them. Often they invited Muslim families to their house for dinner and let the kids enjoy swimming in their pool. This gave the wife the ability to visit with the Muslim woman at her house and talk again at a later time.

One day this missionary asked me to go with him to a Bible study for Jews led by someone he described as an "ex-Jewish lady." My friend said the people would be encouraged to see a Muslim who came to Christ.

This was the first time in my life that I ever had an opportunity to visit a Jewish home. I had never shaken a Jewish person's hand. I never had any personal relationship with a Jewish person.

But I really wanted to go because this was my chance to find out the truth about Jews. At the same time, I was afraid because I really expected all Jewish people to hate me because of my Muslim background. I thought that the people at the prayer meeting would be disrespectful to me or say insulting things about Arabic people. I agreed to go, but I decided ahead of time that if the people treated me poorly, I would just tell my friend, "I'm sorry, but I have to leave." I hoped that I wouldn't have to do this and embarrass my friends.

This was also the first time I had ever heard the term "ex-Jewish."[1] When I came to South Africa, I heard about ex-Muslims for the first time, and I understood that term meant Muslims converted to Christ. But I couldn't understand what ex-Jewish meant because I never imagined that Jewish people could convert to Christianity. It was another new thought for me.

SHAKEN UP BY KINDNESS

When we arrived at the Bible study, the first thing I noticed was the inside of the townhouse where they were meeting. It was beautifully decorated and very clean.

The missionary had contacted Elizabeth, the Jewish young lady who led the Bible study, ahead of time and told her about me. When he introduced me, she was friendly and gave me a hug. I was shocked. This was the first time in my life I had ever been introduced to a Jewish person by name. Throughout my whole life I had avoided any kind of contact with a Jewish person. I actually considered Jews to be less than human. Here I was hugging a Jew as if she were a family member.

I was really shaken up by her kindness. Next my friend introduced me to some of the other Jewish people at the prayer meeting. They were already Christian believers, and they were very friendly. But I paid close attention when he introduced me to a Jewish family that had not accepted Christianity. I wanted to compare the two types of Jewish people.

This Jewish family greeted me and treated me kindly. I couldn't see any hatred or disrespect. I saw them just as human beings and nice people. This went against the picture of Jews that was in my brain from the Quran.

The Lord was really shaking me. I felt as if a volcano were exploding in my brain. The Spirit of God was inside me, convicting me and teaching me.

I was completely silent through the meeting. I just watched people, seeing how they reacted to me.

At the end of the prayer meeting, I asked to speak. I said to Elizabeth, "Jesus' most recent miracle happened here tonight. By this miracle, He united you and me to be brother and sister through His blood. No other power in the world can do this type of reconciliation between the Jews and the Muslims."

She hugged me again, and everybody clapped.

My missionary friends were excited, but they didn't realize how significant this event was in my life. This moment was one of the greatest ways God proved to me that His power was real in my life. He had filled me up with His Spirit so that there was no room in me for hatred toward other people. I could still get upset or angry with an individual, but I didn't hate any more (1 John 2:10–11).

I told my friends that night, "I just wish there were some way my mother or sister could meet this group. I wish they could see the truth about the Jewish people."

MY NEW HEART TOWARD JEWS

I went to the prayer meeting at Elizabeth's house many times. She also visited the missionaries' house. All this time I was seeing proof that what the Quran said about Jews was false. I felt angry about being lied to about a people that had so many good qualities.

I didn't get to finish my two months of outreach with these missionaries. The problem was a book. I had written my testimony and worked hard to translate it into English with a Christian friend. The book was finally printed, and when the Muslim community saw it, they went crazy. Muslims were hunting for me all over Cape Town. They are very aggressive there. After they tried to stab me once, YWAM suggested that I leave the area.

I flew about twelve hundred kilometers back to Johannesburg. I was so happy to be back with my friends who had sponsored my time at YWAM. They were very worried about me getting hurt in Cape Town, but they could also see my new heart. They invited me to speak at a meeting of Messianic Jews, which I did and enjoyed. There I met one of their best friends, a Jewish man who owned a big furniture shop in the mall.

I enjoyed the relationship that I had with this Jewish man, his wife and her sister. My friends and I would have dinner with them from time to time. Or they would invite us to their house. They always included other Messianic Jews whenever we got together.

In this relationship I experienced how the Lord united me with this part of His body—the Messianic Jews. This Jewish family had a heart to witness—not only to Jews but also to *Muslims*. They and my friends passed out copies of my book to Muslims as they were leaving the local mosque after Friday prayers. They also looked for Muslims in the marketplace and gave them books as well.

They put their phone number in the front of the book and wrote, "If you have any questions, please call." The phone calls came, and my friends started to visit these Muslims to tell them about Jesus. They also helped them with practical needs. One group of Muslims had recently immigrated from the Komoros Islands. When winter came, they had no blankets. My friends bought a room full of blankets and passed them out.

I helped with counseling these Muslims. I remember one immigrant from Komoros who was very difficult and hard. He had memorized a lot of the Quran when he was younger. In the end the Lord touched him, and he accepted Jesus. Then he started reaching his own people.

These experiences gave me a great desire to see Muslim converts and Messianic Jews work together to share Jesus with their peoples. It is only through Jesus that we can see a former Muslim speaking to a meeting of Messianic Jews. It is only through Jesus that we can see Messianic Jews going to a mosque to reach out to Muslims.

Jesus Christ is all about reconciliation. He came to show how we can be reconciled with God and also with each other.

I love the words of a letter sent to me by a Jewish man who read one of my books. He wrote:

> Dear Mark,
>
> Thank God for what He has done in your life, and thank you for your stand for the truth. Though my life was not threatened when I put my trust in Jesus (*Yeshua*), I too was met with rejection and disdain. I was raised in a Jewish family.
>
> Both of our peoples need to know Him. He is the only way for true peace and for us to truly love one another. I wish we had more opportunity for Arabic and Jewish believers in Jesus to stand up and be counted and show the world that it is possible.
>
> Your friend in Him,
>
> G.H., Michigan

THE POWER OF GOD

Now you know my story. You can see the power of God at work. You are beginning to get an idea of the stronghold of hatred that is built up inside a Muslim against the Jews. Now I want to take you to the original source of this attitude, which is in the teachings of Islam. In the following pages, you will have a rare opportunity to see what Islam teaches from the Muslim scholar's point of view. This next section will clear up much of the confusion that you have experienced from the media. It will also lay the foundation for you to understand the behavior of Muslims today.

SECTION 2

HOW TO UNDERSTAND WHAT THE QURAN SAYS ABOUT JEWS

CHAPTER 6

The Foundation of Islam

WESTERNERS ARE USED TO BEING LIED to. Isn't that sad? Westerners expect to be lied to by advertising, by salespeople, by business leaders, by politicians, by journalists and others. It's a "hearer beware" world. This is why Westerners are having such a hard time understanding Islam. Someone is not telling the truth—they are sure of that—but they just can't tell who it is.

How can some people call Islam a religion of peace and tolerance while others insist that it is a religion based on force and coercion? Both sides quote the Quran. In this section you will learn the basics of Muslim theology so that you can answer this question for yourself.

We are going to start with some basic facts about Islam, but we will proceed quickly to more specific information.

QURAN AND HADITH

Islam is a religion based on revelations that are said to have been given to the prophet Muhammad by the angel Gabriel. These revelations are called the Quran, and the Quran is considered to be the words of God (Allah) himself. The Quran is written in first person—"I declare this," or "I did that." The *I* in the Quran is Allah. The Quran is the most holy and most authoritative book of Islam.

Islam also relies on the *hadith*, the record of Muhammad's teachings and actions. During Muhammad's life, his followers and some of his wives kept records of what he said and did. Muslim scholars later collected these records, tested their authenticity and organized them into books, which are known all together as the *hadith*. There are six sets of books that are considered to be authoritative. The most trusted set was compiled by a man named al-Bukhari.

Muslims submit to the teachings of the hadith because the Quran commands them to obey Muhammad. There's an interesting story about how Muhammad's authority was first established in the Quran. It involves a Muslim, a Jew, an argument and a murder.

When Muhammad was ruling in Medina, people brought disputes for him to settle. A Muslim man needed someone to judge on a matter between him and a Jewish man. The Jew said, "Let's go to the prophet Muhammad. He'll make a decision."

The Muslim refused and said he wanted to go to Umar ibn al-Khattab, one of Muhammad's military leaders who was known to dislike the Jews.

The Jew agreed, and they went to Umar's house. Umar said, "Don't come to me. Go to the prophet Muhammad."

The Muslim said, "No. I want you to decide."

So Umar said, "Wait," and he went into his house and got a sword. He came out and sliced the Muslim man's neck and killed him.

When the people heard what happened, they were very sad because Muslims were not supposed to kill other Muslims. What would happen to Umar?

Muhammad was sad, too, because Umar was one of his most faithful followers. Then he received another revelation. He told the people, "Rejoice! Allah came to me with verses that set al-Khattab free."[1] This revelation was:

> But no, by your Lord, they can have no Faith, until they make you (O Muhammad) judge in all disputes between them, and find in themselves no resistance against your decision, and accept (them) with full submission.
>
> —SURAH 4:65; SEE ALSO 4:59

In other words, the man who sought a judge other than Muhammad had "no Faith." He was not a Muslim. Therefore, it was OK for Umar to kill him.

When the Muslims heard this Quranic revelation, they rejoiced and danced.

Now, what does this story mean for the practice of Islam? It means that to be a Muslim, you must submit to the judgments, teachings and ways of Muhammad.

Muslims cannot take the words of Allah and reject the words of Muhammad. If anyone denies the prophet Muhammad, then he denies his revelation, which is the basis of Islam. That means that you are not a Muslim. (Remember Surah 4:65 above.)

If a Muslim knows his religion, he knows this. If a person is just Muslim by tradition, then he might not understand this.

The Quran repeats this point more than once. For example:

> He who obeys the Messenger (Muhammad), has indeed obeyed Allah...
>
> —SURAH 4:80

> And whatsoever the Messenger (Muhammad) gives you, take it; and whatsoever he forbids you, abstain (from it).
>
> —SURAH 59:7

> And whoever contradicts and opposes the Messenger (Muhammad) after the right path has been shown clearly to him, and follows other than the believers'

way, We shall keep him in the path he has chosen, and burn him in Hell—what an evil destination![2]

—SURAH 4:115

In the Middle East, the authority of hadith is a part of life. If two people disagree, one might take a copy of the hadith of al-Bukhari in his hands and say, "I swear on the book of Bukhari I am telling the truth."

The hadith is quoted alongside the Quran. When I was in Egypt, the five daily calls to prayer were broadcast over the national radio station and on TV. Before the call, there was recitation from the Quran, and after the call there was recitation from hadith.

You may ask yourself, "Why is this author going through so much trouble to establish the place of hadith in Islam?" The reason is that many people who give an inaccurate picture of Islam do not take into account the teachings of the hadith. They act as if Muhammad does not really represent Islam. From the Muslim point of view, this is heresy.

As you continue to read this book, you are going to learn about Muhammad's beliefs, teachings and actions regarding Jewish people. This isn't just a history lesson. This is the answer to the question about why Muslims cannot get along with Jews right now.

In the next chapter, we are going to see how Muhammad saw Islam in relationship to the religions in Arabia that were already worshiping one God—Christianity and Judaism.

CHAPTER 7

Islam's Relationship to Judaism and Christianity

A LWAYS, ALWAYS, ALWAYS KEEP IN MIND that Muhammad lived in the seventh century A.D. At that time, the Jews had been worshiping Yahweh for almost twenty-five hundred years. The Christians had been following Jesus for six hundred years. Where did the Islamic system of belief fit in?

Muhammad had a very powerful way of fitting in. He basically said to the Jews and Christians, "Your prophets were prophets of Islam. Your God is the same as the God of Islam."

> Our *Ilah* (God) and your *Ilah* (God) is One.
> —SURAH 29:46; SEE ALSO SURAH 3:64

How can this be? How could the prophets of the Bible be preaching Islam when the first time the world heard of Islam was through Muhammad's revelations in the seventh century?

The Quran says that Islam came *before* Judaism and Christianity; it was the religion practiced by Abraham.

> Ibrahim (Abraham) was neither a Jew nor a Christian, but he was a true Muslim...Verily, among mankind who have the best claim to Ibrahim (Abraham) are those who followed him, and this Prophet (Muhammad) and those who have believed (Muslims).
> —SURAH 3:67–68

The Quran refers to Islam as the "religion of Abraham"

many times (Surah 2:130, 135; 3:95; 4:125; 6:161). Also, Abraham and many prophets after him preached Islam, including Isaac, Ishmael, Jacob, Joseph, Noah, David, Solomon, Moses, John and Jesus (Surah 4:163; 6:84–86). (Appendix A explains the role of Abraham in Islam.)

So how does Islam explain the existence of Judaism and Christianity? The Quran teaches that Judaism and Christianity were based on the "earlier revelations" about Allah that came from the prophets (meaning revelations that came earlier than the Quran). These earlier revelations were the Jewish Scriptures and the Christian New Testament. However, according to Islam, the Jews and Christians corrupted their Scriptures and were no longer worshiping Allah properly, so Allah had to send a fresh revelation by way of Muhammad.

According to Islam, Muhammad's revelations canceled out Christianity and Judaism and brought people back to the one true religion that Abraham understood and practiced (Islam).[1]

MUHAMMAD IS THE FINAL PROPHET

Islam teaches that Allah rejected the children of Israel because of their sins, and God went back to the seed of Abraham and chose a person from the line of Ishmael to be the final prophet. (See Appendix A.)

Muhammad gave clear teachings about how he saw his position among the prophets of Islam. Muhammad said:

> My similitude in comparison with the other Prophets before me is that of a man who has built a house nicely and beautifully, except for a place of one brick in a corner. The people go round about it and wonder at its beauty, but say: "Would that this brick be put in its place!" So I am that brick, and I am the last (end) of the Prophets.[2]

Furthermore, Allah decreed that those who followed Muhammad's revelation would become the new chosen people.

> You [true believers in Islamic Monotheism, and real followers of Prophet Muhammad and his *Sunnah*] are the best of peoples ever raised up for mankind…
>
> —SURAH 3:110

This verse goes on to say:

> …had the people of the Scripture (Jews and Christians) believed, it would have been better for them.

Islam teaches that Muslims now have God's favor, not the Jews. Muslims are honored because they are fulfilling their responsibility of carrying Allah's final message to the world as given to the final prophet, Muhammad.[3]

PARADISE EARNED BY WORKS

What does it mean to be a Muslim? It means that you submit your will to the will of Allah. Being a Muslim is more than accepting a set of beliefs. You are a Muslim by your actions.

Muhammad said in hadith, "The contents of the heart are reflected in good works." In other words, it's not enough to say you are a Muslim by your tongue. You have to do good works.

The Quran teaches that after a person dies, he goes to the grave and remains there until the Day of Judgment. At that time the person will go before Allah, who will put his good works and bad works on a scale. Then Allah will decide if that person can go to Paradise. The Quran says:

> This Day (Day of Resurrection), none will be wronged in anything, nor will you be requited anything except that which you used to do.
>
> —SURAH 36:54

FIVE PILLARS OF ISLAM

You often hear about the five pillars of Islam. These are the foundation of the good works that Islam says will please Allah. These pillars are:

1. *Confess that none but Allah has the right to be worshiped and that Muhammad is his messenger.* When you convert to Islam, you must make this declaration, but that is not the end of it. Muslims are reminded of this confession five times a day because it is included in the call for prayer.

2. *Perform prayers five times a day.* If you don't pray five times a day, but you still believe that you should, then you have sinned, but you haven't left Islam. If you say that you don't believe in doing five prayers a day, then you have left Islam.

3. *Give alms* (zakat). Alms are usually calculated as a percentage of income, approximately 2.5 percent. In modern times, a Muslim can choose to give the *zakat* according to his personal preferences. He can give to the local mosque, directly to the needy or to people in his own family who need help. Some people choose to give to charities that support fanatic groups. Bin Laden and al Qaeda were funded by millions of dollars in alms from the rich people in Gulf countries.[4] Rich people spend a lot on alms, especially helping the poor during the month of Ramadan. My father would feed the evening "break fast" meal to eight hundred to a thousand poor people in front of his factory during Ramadan.

He set up tables and chairs and had food catered from local restaurants. That would be twenty-five thousand to thirty thousand meals during Ramadan month. This kind of charity is practiced throughout Muslim countries.

4. *Make a pilgrimage (*hajj*) to Mecca once in a lifetime if finances allow.* The Quran says, *"Hajj* (pilgrimage to Makkah) to the House *(Ka'bah)* is a duty that mankind owes to Allah, those who can afford the expenses (for one's conveyance, provision and residence); and whoever disbelieves [i.e. denies *Hajj* (pilgrimage to Makkah), then he is a disbeliever of Allah]..." (Surah 3:97). More than three million Muslims make the pilgrimage to Mecca, Saudi Arabia, each year during the third month after Ramadan. So many people go there all at once that there are not enough hotel rooms for them, and many sleep in tents. When I was a Muslim, I made this pilgrimage one time, and I performed the prescribed duties—always in a throng of thousands and thousands of people.

5. *Fast during the holy month of Ramadan.* For committed Muslims, this means not eating from 4 A.M. until the sun sets. If you are traveling or too sick to fast, you can make up the days that you missed. If you don't fast during Ramadan because you lack will power, it's a sin, but you can be pardoned. On the other hand, if you don't fast during Ramadan because you don't believe in it, then you are out of Islam. You cannot be a Muslim and deny fasting during Ramadan.

Although it is not described as a pillar, *jihad* (fighting in the name of Allah) is one of the greatest things you can do to please Allah. I will explain more about jihad in chapter eight. (You can also get more details from my book *Islam and Terrorism*.)

WAYS TO DISPLEASE ALLAH

Now let's look at the things that Islam says will displease Allah.

1. The worst thing you can do is to *believe in a god other than Allah* or to believe in Allah but also believe in other gods at the same time. For example, a Muslim could never say, "I believe in Allah and the Quran, but I also believe Jesus is the Son of God." That would be ascribing a partner to Allah, and it is a sin that won't be forgiven (Surah 4:116).

2. *Insulting Muhammad*, the prophet of Islam (Surah 4:65, 115).

3. *Neglecting any of the five pillars.*

4. *Breaking Islamic law,* which includes prohibitions against drinking alcohol, engaging in immoral sexual behavior, eating pork, charging interest for loans, gambling and other laws.

5. *Running away from jihad* (Surah 8:16).

Before Judgment Day, a Muslim cannot know for sure whether Allah will be pleased with him. However, Islamic teaching does say Muslims can get forgiveness for some sins by fasting during Ramadan and by going on the pilgrimage to Mecca.

I hope that you recognize that Muslim behavior in many

different areas of life is a result of the people's belief that their works will be weighed and judged by Allah.[5]

CONCLUSION

From this overview of Islam, I hope you remember the following:

* Islam claims to worship the same God as the Jews and the Christians.

* At the same time, Islam claims to have superseded Judaism and Christianity. Therefore, in order to worship the one true God, you must practice Islam.

* Muhammad claimed to be the final prophet of Allah.

* Islam requires people to earn their way into Paradise by works.

This knowledge lays the foundation you need to understand Islam's teaching about the Jews.

CHAPTER 8

Does the Quran Call for Tolerance or Holy War?

NOW LET'S ANSWER THE QUESTION WE had at the beginning of the section: How can people claim that the Quran teaches two opposite things?

* Tolerance toward non-Muslims
* Holy war against non-Muslims

The key to answering this question is to remember how the Quran was revealed. Muhammad said that the angel Gabriel would come to him from time to time and reveal verses. This process occurred over a period of about twenty-two years. The revelations were often directly related to what was occurring in Muhammad's life at the time.

Muhammad's life can be divided into two parts—the tolerant years in Mecca and the aggressive years in Medina. The revelations Muhammad received in Medina sometimes clashed with the ones from Mecca. As you will learn, Muhammad received revelations that told the Muslims how to handle these contradictions.

Let's look first at Muhammad's "tolerant years."

THE TOLERANT YEARS

Muhammad was living in Mecca when he first began to receive revelations in 610. At this time he was a preacher, trying to win people to Islam by being nice. Even after he and his followers were persecuted and moved to the nearby city of Medina in 622, Muhammad continued to preach a positive message for about a year, hoping to attract people to Islam that way.

> Let there be no compulsion in religion: Truth stands out clear from Error: whoever rejects Evil and believes in Allah has grasped the most trustworthy hand-hold, that never breaks. And Allah hears and knows all things.
>
> —SURAH 2:256, ALI TRANSLATION

This verse essentially says, "You can't force anybody to change their religion. The right way should be obvious." People who say Islam is a religion of peace point to this verse.[1] However, they need to take into account that this verse was only an early installment of the revelations Muhammad received regarding those who rejected Islam.

Muhammad was presenting a peaceful religion at this time—a good strategy because he had only a few followers and they were all very vulnerable. But Islam didn't stay weak.

THE AGGRESSIVE YEARS

When he first arrived in Medina, Muhammad continued to try to persuade people with words alone. This lasted for about a year, during which Muhammad converted many of the idol worshipers but almost none of the Jews. Then Muhammad launched a new strategy, a strategy based on power. This is when he declared jihad (holy war) and went out to convert nonbelievers to Islam by the sword. One of his new revelations stated:

> Kill the *Mushrikun* [pagans] wherever you find them, and capture them and besiege them, and lie in wait for them in each and every ambush.
>
> —SURAH 9:5

This "verse of the sword," as it is now known, contradicted earlier revelations like Surah 2:256 above. However, a verse was revealed to Muhammad in Medina that justified the inconsistency.

> Whatever a Verse (revelation) do We abrogate or cause to be forgotten, We bring a better one or similar to it. Know you not that Allah is able to do all things?
>
> —SURAH 2:106

This verse says that Allah causes some parts of the Quran to be abrogated. *Abrogate* means "to abolish by authoritative action," "to treat as nonexistent" or "to nullify." These "abrogated" verses are replaced by verses that are "better" or "similar."

The practical application of this principle is that when there is a contradiction between two verses in the Quran, the newer revelation overrides the previous revelation. The new cancels the old.

You can still read the words, "There is no compulsion in religion," in the Quran, but they no longer have authority. This verse has been *mansookh* (canceled) by revelations that came later.

JEWS AND CHRISTIANS CHALLENGED MUHAMMAD

Jews and Christians were watching Muhammad's teachings carefully. When they saw him change his teachings, they criticized him: "How can you be from God? What god changes his mind? How can you say one verse today and then cancel it tomorrow?"

Their complaints are mentioned in the Quran.

> And when We change a Verse (of the Quran,) in place of another—and Allah knows best what He sends down—they (the disbelievers) say: "You (O

Muhammad) are but a *Muftari!* (forger, liar)." Nay, but most them know not.

—SURAH 16:101

In the next verse, Allah told Muhammad how to answer these accusations.

Say (O Muhammad) *Ruh-ul-Qudus* [Jibril (Gabriel)] has brought it (the Quran) down from your Lord with truth, and it may make firm and strengthen (the Faith of) those who believe, and as a guidance and glad tidings to those who have submitted (to Allah as Muslims).

—SURAH 16:102

In other words, Allah told Muhammad to simply say that the Quran is true, it came from God, and it is for the benefit of those who believe in it. This was the answer about why some new revelations were contradicting some old revelations.

DO ALL MUSLIMS INTERPRET THE QURAN THIS WAY?

Now you should be asking yourself, Do all Muslims interpret the Quran this way? Do all Muslims accept that a contradiction in the Quran is solved by using the newest revelation?

This principle is known in Arabic as *nasikh.* It means that Allah led Muhammad in a progressive revelation.

Nasikh is widely accepted in Islam. The two largest sects in Islam, Sunni and Shia, accept this principle. I learned it at my Muslim high school. I also studied it at Al-Azhar University in Quranic commentary class. I taught it at the mosque where I preached.

Many copies of the Quran have a table that shows whether a surah is from Mecca or Medina in order to help readers know which is a newer revelation.

Even Quranic history shows that *nasikh* is valid. If there

were no *nasikh,* Muhammad's followers would have just stayed with Mecca ideals. There would have been no jihad and no Islamic military to conquer land and people all over the world. Islam would have never left Arabia.

The problem is, if you do not accept *nasikh*, how are you going to interpret the Quran? Are you going to just choose the verses you like best? And what are you going to do about the example of Muhammad? He did more than just preach in Mecca. He went to Medina and declared war on unbelievers. Are you going to follow just half of his example?

If anyone denies the continuing revelation of Allah to Muhammad, they are denying Islam itself. Some Muslims who are not well taught in their faith may not understand *nasikh* fully, but it is still a foundational principle of Islam.

CHAPTER 9

The "Nice Islam" of the West

THE ATTACK AGAINST THE UNITED STATES on September 11, 2001 caused major damage to the image of Islam. Islam is now like a wounded lion trying to stay alive. Muslim leaders, particularly in the West, are focusing on damage control, trying to present a different image of Islam.

I frequently speak on university campuses, sometimes at the invitation of Christian groups and sometimes by my own initiative at Muslim meetings. Twice I have seen pamphlets titled "Some Misconceptions About Islam." These pamphlets are always filled with verses from Mecca, presenting a version of Islam that sounds more like Christianity than Islam. Some who practice Islam sincerely believe these teachings are true. But well-educated Islamic leaders know that these teachings are part of a strategy to make Islam look good to Westerners.

In this chapter, I want to respond to these teachings. Not only do Muslims use them, but often Westerners pick them up and unwittingly perpetuate them as well.

WHAT IS A JUSTIFIED WAR?

While speaking at a university in the United States, I heard a familiar challenge. "Muhammad had to fight because he was defending his revelation and his people. His battles were

51

justified." Those who say Islam is a religion of peace often argue that Muslims are only permitted to fight a justified war.[1]

The question of what makes a justified war made me think of the wars that Muhammad and his successors fought. How were they justified? I answered the student this way:

> What did my country Egypt do to Muhammad that he came and ruined my country? Egypt never attacked Muslims, but the Islamic army came and killed more than four million Egyptians during the first century of Islam.[2]
>
> Muslims did not stop after Egypt; they went south to Sudan and west to conquer all of North Africa. What did the countries of North Africa do to provoke Muhammad or his successors? Nothing.
>
> What danger was Spain, Portugal and Southern Europe to Muhammad and his successors? Islam attacked them, too.
>
> The Quran commands Muslims to go and rule the entire world and submit all mankind to the religion of Islam. That is the basis of war in Islam.

Let's look at where people are getting the term "justified war." It stems partly from Surah 17:33:

> And do not kill anyone whose killing Allah has forbidden, except for a just cause. And whoever is killed wrongfully... We have given his heir the authority [to demand *Qisas*—Law of Equality in punishment—or to forgive, or to take *Diyah* (blood money)].

I would like to point out that this verse is not talking about war. It refers to a murder that is committed in society. The verse goes on to describe the rights of the victim's family. It is part of a passage in the Quran that gave guidelines for daily life, such as honoring parents, giving to the poor, sexual morality and the treatment of orphans, among other things.

Since this verse is not about war, it does not impact the many other verses in the Quran that speak of jihad.

ARE THEY LYING OR DREAMING?

Here's another type of question I often hear. A man at one of my meetings was holding a newspaper. In it was a quote from the imam of a local mosque who had said that Islam is a religion of peace. "How can he say this?" the man asked.

I don't know this imam personally, but his statement comes from one of two motives:

1. *Wishful thinking.* He really believes that Islam should be about peace, so he preaches the peaceful side of Islam. He sincerely believes he is practicing Islam, but peace is not the final revelation of Islam.

2. *Deception.* Some imams will try to make Islam look attractive to Westerners. In other words, they know the truth about Islam, but they disguise it in order to appeal to more people. The interesting thing is that in Islam a Muslim may *profess* to deny *nasikh* if doing so is for the purpose of protecting the image of Islam and furthering missionary activity. This is particularly acceptable if the Muslim is living as a minority in a non-Muslim country (such as the United States). But this denial must be in words only. In their hearts, Muslims must continue to accept *nasikh* and follow the full and final development of the Quranic revelation.

Either way, this imam is not telling the truth, and he is just adding to the confusion about Islam.

TELLING HALF THE STORY

Now let's look at what some Western writers have been saying.

High schools and universities have been using a best-selling book titled *Islam: A Short History*. This book says, "Muhammad never asked Jews or Christians to accept Islam unless they particularly wished to do so, because they had received perfectly valid revelations of their own."[3] As support, the author quoted Surah 29:46:

> And argue not with the people of the Scripture (Jews and Christians), unless it be in (a way) that is better (with good words and in good manner, inviting them to Islamic Monotheism with His Verses), except with such of them as do wrong; and say (to them): "We believe in that which has been revealed to us and revealed to you; our *Ilah* (God) and your *Ilah* (God) is One (i.e. Allah), and to Him we have submitted (as Muslims)."

This verse sounds like tolerance embodied. The problem is that this verse is a Mecca revelation. As such it is canceled out by the verse of the sword, which is a Medina revelation (Surah 9:5).

When I read a statement that says, "Muhammad *never* asked Jews or Christians to accept Islam," I really wonder about the author's motives. Is this statement made out of a lack of understanding, or is it the result of pushing a specific agenda?

The books about Islam that are written in English seem designed to make Islam look nice. They are often written by Western scholars who quote other books written in English. These people have read about Islam, but they have not experienced it.

One of the most deceptive ways I have seen of presenting Islam is to leave out the Medina revelations altogether. That is the strategy taken by a book called *Approaching the Qur'an: The Early Revelations.*[4]

What is most disturbing is that this book was approved as mandatory reading for all freshman students entering the University of North Carolina for fall of 2002. No wonder Americans are so confused about what Islam really teaches!

SUMMARY AND CONCLUSION

You now know some of the basic facts about Islam. You are also equipped to deal with some of the confusing messages you have been hearing in the media and in popular books about Islam written in the English language.

You are probably now wondering about your friends, neighbors, coworkers and acquaintances who are Muslims. Do they really believe what I have just described? I will answer that question in the next chapter.

CHAPTER 10

Does My Muslim Neighbor Believe in Jihad?

P EOPLE IN THE West ARE VERY curious about the differences between Muslims. They see that some Muslims
join radical groups and attack innocent people while others
live quiet lives as business owners in the West. They find it
hard to imagine that their nice Muslim neighbors or
coworkers believe all the teachings of the Quran and support
Muhammad's practice of holy war.

There are between 6 million and 8 million Muslims living
in the United States. Most of these are immigrants from
Middle Eastern countries. The next largest group is black
American converts. The smallest group is white American
converts. Outside of the United States, there are 1.2 billion
more Muslims. From my observations and experience, both
in the United States and in other countries, Muslims can be
divided into three main groups.

ORDINARY MUSLIMS

Ordinary Muslims practice some of the teachings of Islam,
but they don't want to do anything difficult, like participate
in jihad. They are more interested in having nice lives, providing for their children and running their businesses. They
are Muslims because of their culture and tradition rather
than because of strong religious beliefs.

Most of the Muslims in the United States are ordinary Muslims. Some even send their children to Christian schools. Even in the Middle East there are more ordinary Muslims than committed Muslims. It would take time and motivation to turn ordinary Muslims into committed Muslims.

From the point of view of a committed Muslim, this group should be referred to as secular Muslims because they are not submitting wholly to Islam.[1]

COMMITTED MUSLIMS

Committed Muslims are making great efforts to live according to Islam. They are praying five times a day, giving alms and fasting during Ramadan. A committed Muslim may not be in a radical group like Hamas, but he could choose to cross that line at any time that he feels his religion or people are threatened.

Orthodox Muslims

A subset of committed Muslims is the orthodox Muslims. Not only do orthodox Muslims want to follow the requirements of Islam, but they also want to do it in the same way as Muhammad did in the seventh century. They spend much time reading the Quran and Islamic books. Following the Quran and hadith, they may put severe restrictions on women. In Islamic countries, orthodox Muslims may choose to grow out their beards, but in the West they may not look different from other Muslims.

Sufites

This is the first sect in Islam that tried to transfer the meaning of jihad from spreading Islam with the sword to a spiritual struggle to fight evil within oneself. Sufism started six centuries after Muhammad's death. Only 2 to 3 percent of Muslims worldwide are Sufites. Orthodox Muslims and fanatic Muslims reject them and do not consider them to be true Muslims.

FANATIC MUSLIMS

These are committed Muslims who put their words into action. They are the types of people who join militant groups such as Hamas or work with al-Qaeda. They are ready to practice jihad (to kill or be killed in the name of Islam).

HOW TO TELL THE DIFFERENCE

After the September 11 attacks, you could identify the different types of Muslims according to their reactions. The ordinary Muslims were pretty quiet. In the United States, they were even hanging American flags on their houses and showing support for the United States.

The committed Muslims in the Middle East were demonstrating in the streets in support of al-Qaeda.

The fanatic Muslims were thrilled with the victory and were making new attacks, such as the kidnapping and murder of journalist Daniel Pearl, and other attacks that are still continuing.

Attitudes toward Jews

Now let's look at how these groups feel toward the state of Israel and Jewish people.

The ordinary Muslim has negative feelings toward Jews because of both his culture and his religion. He would never receive a Jewish person in his house, he wouldn't trust them in business, and he would never think of being friends with a Jewish person. Ordinary Muslims really believe that Jews are evil people who should be avoided.

This was demonstrated by a Gallup poll taken in nine Muslim countries during December 2001 and January 2002. Almost ten thousand personal interviews were conducted.

One question was about the identities of the hijackers.

Although U.S. officials say all nineteen of the September 11 hijackers were Arab men, only 18 percent of those polled in six Islamic countries say they believe Arabs carried out the attacks; 61 percent say Arabs were not responsible; and 21 percent say they don't know.[2]

If these people do not think Arabs were responsible, then who did it? One persistent rumor is that Jews were somehow behind it all. The rumor said that four thousand Jewish workers at the World Trade Center called in sick on September 11 because they had been warned in advance of the attack.[3]

A committed Muslim holds all these same prejudices against Jews. He also understands his religious beliefs in a deeper way and therefore knows the teachings in the Quran against the Jews.

The fanatic Muslim justifies many of his actions based on the fact the Jewish state exists. He blames his terrorist activity on the Jews. He makes Jews his target. In the videotaped murder of journalist Daniel Pearl, his killers forced him to begin with a brief, factually correct description of his roots: "My father's Jewish. My mother's Jewish. I'm Jewish."[4]

WHAT DO THESE CATEGORIES MEAN?

These categories mean that not all Muslims have the same level of knowledge and commitment. Some ordinary Muslims may not even know about the things that you are about to read. They have a general idea that Jews persecuted Muhammad and wanted to destroy his revelation, but they can't tell it in detail.

Committed and fanatic Muslims know these stories and use them to shape their beliefs.

Now you are going to see for yourself how the example of

Muhammad and the early Muslims provides a blueprint for the attitudes and actions of Muslims today. When you are finished, you will have a much clearer picture of why Islam is against Israel.

Section 3

Phase One of the Unfinished Battle: Muhammad Seeks Jewish Converts (610–623)

CHAPTER 11

Setting the Stage

J UST BEFORE HIS DEATH, JESUS ENTERED Jerusalem riding
on a young donkey. The people and His disciples joyfully
praised God, but the Jewish religious leaders tried to stop
them. Jesus told them, "I tell you . . . if they keep quiet, the
stones will cry out" (v. 40). Then Jesus spoke His final
prophecy over Jerusalem before His death. With weeping
and tears, He looked out over the city and cried out:

> If you, even you, had only known on this day what
> would bring you peace—but now it is hidden from
> your eyes. The days will come upon you when your ene-
> mies will build an embankment against you and
> encircle you and hem you in on every side. They will
> dash you to the ground, you and the children within
> your walls. They will not leave one stone on another,
> because you did not recognize the time of God's
> coming to you.
>
> —LUKE 19:41–44

Imagine Jesus standing there weeping as He foresaw the
pain and suffering of His people.

About thirty-seven years later the prophecy of Jesus was
fulfilled when the Roman leader Titus came and destroyed
Jerusalem, and the Jews dispersed throughout the world to
escape the persecution of the Romans. A large group of

them went to Arabia, and they settled in the valleys and different cities in Arabia. They spent exactly five hundred years working hard in agriculture and business, becoming known for the swords, knives and tents they produced. They worked very hard and made good products that the Bedouins and Arabs bought from them.

The success of the Jewish community in Arabia was well known throughout the Middle East. The Jews built many synagogues.

The Jewish community in that time never dreamed there would be a repeat of the history of the bloody Roman leader Titus, who destroyed their cities and land in Israel five hundred years earlier. This time it would be an Arabic man who played the role of ruining the life of the Jewish community.

MUHAMMAD'S BIRTH AND EARLY LIFE

In the Arabian Desert in the year 570, a baby boy was born. Life was hard in Arabia, and this little boy's father died even before his birth. His mother took the baby and went to live with her family.

When the boy was six years old, his mother got a high fever, and within just a few days, she too had died. His grandfather on his father's side took over care of the child, but again, the arrangement did not last. When he was still a young boy, the grandfather died. This time his care was transferred to his uncle on his father's side, and he went to live with his cousins.

The young boy tended sheep. When he was a teenager he started traveling with his uncle who was in business as a caravan trader. One time his uncle took him along on a business trip to Syria, where he met a Nestorian priest.* This false priest

---

* The Nestorian cult came out of Christianity and denied the Trinity and Jesus as the Son of God. It was popular in the area of Syria.

noticed a little birthmark on the boy's shoulder. He said to his uncle, "Behold, this child is going to be the final prophet for our world. This is the stamp of prophethood." Then he warned, "Don't let the Jews hear about this or see this birthmark on his shoulder. If they find out, they will try to kill him."[1]

This was the first time the boy ever thought Jews were a threat to his life. What a horrible influence this advice had on that little boy. It was the foundation of his later attitude toward all the Jewish communities of Arabia.

When the boy became a man, he got a job working for a camel caravan. He was promoted and finally became the caravan leader. He led camel caravans to places like Syria and Yemen to exchange goods.

The camel caravan was owned by the wealthiest, most powerful woman of the area. She was over forty, four times divorced, and had children. In contrast, her caravan manager was a young man of twenty-five and employed by her. But she proposed (very uncommon for Arabic society), and they were married.

The young man was Muhammad bin Abdullah, now known as the prophet of Islam. The wealthy caravan owner was Khadija. Fifteen years after their marriage, Muhammad was meditating in a cave when a being who called himself the angel Gabriel appeared to him. This revelation was the beginning of Islam.

MUHAMMAD'S CITY

Let's look at the city in which Muhammad lived—Mecca. This city still exists in present-day Saudi Arabia. The people who lived in Mecca during Muhammad's time were:

* Mostly Arabic tribes practicing primitive religions, such as idol worship.

* A small group of Jews practicing Judaism. Even though they were small in numbers, they had a high standing in society because they were rich from business.

* Members of the Abionite cult. This cult came out of Christianity. They followed the rules of the Bible, but they did not believe Jesus could take away their sins, and they did not believe in the Trinity. There were just a few hundred Abionites in Mecca.

At that time, there were great problems in the Christian church both in the West and the East caused by the many heresies in the church. There were two types of Christian people in Arabia—the true Christians, who were living mostly in Yemen and the area of Jordan, and the false Christians, including the Abionites and the Nestorians.

The Christian church treated the Abionites and Nestorians very harshly. The orthodox churches rejected them, exposed their false teaching and preached against them.

There was also great friction between Christianity and Judaism. Christians complained that the Jews killed the Messiah. The Jews countered that Messiah had not yet come, so they couldn't have killed him.

Despite the religious conflicts among Christians and Jews, there were no big problems between Arabs and Jews. Isn't it amazing to think that before Islam, Arabs and Jews got along with each other?

MUHAMMAD'S REACTION TO RELIGION

As a child, Muhammad gained an inside understanding of the idol worship of his day. His grandfather, who cared for him briefly, was the caretaker of Al-Kaaba, which meant he handled cleaning and repairs. Al-Kaaba, located in Mecca, was the regional center of idol worship. People came from all over Arabia to worship there. Each tribe had an idol in the temple. After his grandfather died, care of Al-Kaaba passed to his son, which was the uncle who also assumed care of Muhammad. The privilege of caring for Al-Kaaba had been passed down for many generations. So Muhammad went to Al-Kaaba frequently. He saw the people bowing down to these statues, and he saw the businessmen who made a living by making and selling the statues. The leading tribe of Mecca (Quraysh) financially benefited from it all.

I believe this situation created a type of resistance in the heart of Muhammad. It pushed Muhammad to establish his own way of searching for God. He swore that when he grew up he would never bow down to one of the idols that existed throughout Mecca and Arabia at that time.[2]

LEARNING FROM THE JEWS AND CHRISTIANS

Muhammad sought people out to discuss their views of God. He became greatly influenced by the Abionites through his wife, Khadija, who was a part of this cult.[3] Khadija's cousin Waraqua bin Naufal was an Abionite priest and an influential religious leader in Mecca. He became Muhammad's mentor, teaching him about Christianity. The teaching from the New Testament was probably focused on the Book of Matthew, because that is the only part of the New Testament that was available in Arabic at that time (according to Christian historians).

This priest also taught Muhammad about the faith of the Jews. The Old Testament teaching was probably focused on the Torah (the first five books of the Old Testament written by Moses) and the Psalms, which were called the Songs of David. From these books, Muhammad would have learned how the people of Israel were God's chosen people.

Muhammad also had contact with the Jews in Mecca as a part of his business transactions working for the caravan.

As a young man, Muhammad began traveling to a little cave in one of the mountains surrounding the city of Mecca to spend time praying to the unseen god, seeking to see the face of the God-creator. He would spend one, two or three days at a time in prayer. His wife, Khadija, would bring him water and food. He spent more than fifteen years doing this. Then, in 610 the first revelation came. Soon Muhammad began preaching Islam in his home city of Mecca.

THE FIRST YEAR AT MEDINA

Muhammad gained converts in Mecca, but they were persecuted. He and his little group of believers fled from Mecca to Medina, which is a very significant event in Islamic history. A small group of people welcomed him in Medina, and Muhammad set out to win more converts.

Let's take a moment to look at the way Muhammad achieved his goals. Muhammad grew up without a mother or father, so he had very little stability in his life. When he had an opportunity to be married to Khadija, he saw many benefits—wealth, influence, stability—so he accepted it. In other words, Muhammad looked for people and resources to meet his goals. When he went to Medina, he found ways to acquire those resources peacefully in the beginning.

First Muhammad addressed the two most powerful tribes, who had been involved in a cruel war against each other for many years, with many deaths on both sides. He set out to win them over. When they were converted to Islam and no longer at war, he set his sights on the power and influence of the Jewish community.

Medina was home to the largest Jewish community in Arabia at that time. When Muhammad lived there, he interacted with Jews every day. He did business with them, even buying some of the swords that the Jewish craftsmen were famous for. He visited their homes and ate with them.

Muhammad believed that converting the Jewish people to Islam would provide powerful assets to support his revelation. He recognized the benefits of their finances and their established theology. He also expected that Jewish converts would be persuasive missionaries for Islam. He planned for them to debate other Jews for him and to convert them. He also wanted the Jewish converts to use their skills to convince the idol worshipers to follow Islam.

So, in the first year in Medina, Muhammad didn't want to conquer, punish or enslave Jews. He wanted to entice Jews to be "on his team," so to speak. Therefore, he needed to make Islam attractive. Quranic revelations from this time in Medina presented a positive attitude toward the Jews.

The Quran reflected many of the teachings of Judaism, such as washing before prayer, fasting, allowing divorce, no consumption of pork and the law of retribution (eye for an eye, tooth for a tooth, Surah 5:45). In deference to the Jews, Muhammad also commanded his followers to turn toward Jerusalem when they prayed.

CHAPTER 12

The Quran's Nice Words About Jews

I WANT TO GIVE YOU A BALANCED, honest picture of what the Quran says about the Jews. It's not all bad. During the first half of his revelations, Muhammad received several favorable words about Jews. The five most important ones are listed below.

1. The Jews are Allah's only chosen people.

> O Children of Israel! Remember My Favour which I bestowed upon you and that I preferred you to the 'Alamin [mankind and jinn* (of your time period, in the past)].
> —SURAH 2:47, SEE ALSO VERSE 122; CF. GENESIS 13; 17

2. Allah protected the Jews when they were living as strangers in a foreign land.

> Verily, Fir'aun (Pharaoh) exalted himself in the land and made its people sects, weakening (oppressing) a group (i.e. Children of Israel) among them: killing their sons, and letting their females live. Verily, he was of the *Mufsidun* (i.e. those who commit great sins and crimes, oppressors, tyrants).
> And We wished to do a favour to those who were

---

* According to Islam, *jinn* are one of Allah's creations, not human and not angel.

> weak (and oppressed) in the land, and to make them
> rulers and to make them the inheritors, and to establish
> them in the land, and We let Fir'aun (Pharaoh) and
> Haman and their hosts receive from them that which
> they feared.

—Surah 28:4–6

Through these verses Muhammad reminded the Jewish community about the story of their grandfather Joseph in Egypt and what happened to them through the years of slavery and persecution. Muhammad presented these stories as Quranic revelations to convince the Jews that their God was the same as the God of the Quran. These stories were meant to show that Allah remembered his chosen people and cared for them and wanted them to believe in Muhammad and to accept his revelation.

Muhammad presented nothing new. The story was already in the Bible. The Jewish community already knew it.

3. Allah chose all his prophets from the Jewish people.

> And (remember) when *Musa* (Moses) said to his people:
> "O my people! Remember the Favour of Allah to you
> when He made Prophets among you, made you kings
> and gave you what He had not given to any other…"

—Surah 5:20

The Quran says that Allah honored Jewish people and chose all his prophets from them and made them kings and gave them riches.

There are many other verses that talk about the Jewish prophets. The surah titled The Prophets (Surah 21) speaks about Abraham, Noah, David, Solomon, Job, Ishmael, Enoch, Isaiah and Jonah. It also mentions John the Baptist and ends with the story of the virgin Mary and her pregnancy with the Lord Jesus Christ.

4. Allah would be kind to Jews (and Christians) who believed in one God and performed good works.

> Verily! Those who believe and those who are Jews and Christians, and Sabians,* whoever believes in Allah and the Last Day and does righteous good deeds shall have their reward with their Lord, on them shall be no fear, nor shall they grieve.
>
> —SURAH 2:62; CF. SURAH 5:69

This verse did not require Christians and Jews to accept Muhammad or Islam as the one true religion. It actually asked them only to do what they were already doing: 1) believe in God (referred to as Allah); 2) believe in the last day or the Day of Judgment; and 3) do good works. If they did that, the Quran said Allah would judge them kindly.

This verse was an affirmation for Jews and Christians, a way to build a positive relationship between Muhammad and the other religions of the area that were worshiping one god.

In this verse, Jews and Christians were not accused of being infidels and enemies of Allah. That rhetoric would come in the second phase of Muhammad's revelation.

5. Allah would bless Jews (and Christians) who practiced the teachings of their holy books.

> Verily, We did send down the Taurat (Torah) [to Musa (Moses)], therein was guidance and light, by which the Prophets, who submitted themselves to Allah's Will, judged for the Jews.
>
> —SURAH 5:44; CF. VERSES 46–47

If only they had stood fast by the Law, the Gospel, and all the revelation that was sent to them from their Lord,

---

* The word *Sabian* in Arabic refers to someone who worshiped God and then turned to false beliefs. In this verse it refers to a specific group of people, some of whom are still living in Northeast Iraq today.

they would have enjoyed happiness from every side.[1]
—SURAH 5:66, ALI TRANSLATION

In the above verse, the Quran says that the Jews and Christians received their Scriptures from God. If they applied their own Scriptures to their lives, the Quran says that they would be blessed.

CONCLUSION

The most important thing to remember from this chapter is that all during his time in Mecca, and for the first year in Medina, Muhammad tried to make Islam attractive to Jews. In the beginning, Muhammad's goal was to find common ground with the Jews. He wanted to encourage them to accept Islam on the basis that it was the true religion that Abraham practiced. However, the Jews did not respond in the way Muhammad had hoped. In the next section we will see how Muhammad reacted.

SECTION 4

PHASE TWO OF THE UNFINISHED BATTLE: MUHAMMAD PUNISHES THE JEWS FOR REJECTING HIM (623–632)

CHAPTER 13

Jews Resist Muhammad's Claims to Their God and Their Scriptures

IMAGINE YOU ARE A JEWISH PERSON living in Medina during the time of the prophet of Islam (around 623). You are a craftsman who makes swords and knives, and you are a wealthy, accepted member of society.

One day you hear people talking about Muhammad, the caravan leader. You are familiar with him because he buys some of the swords and knives you make. He says he has new revelations about the one true God. You wonder, *Could Muhammad be the Messiah, the one we have been waiting for?*

So, you go to hear him teach in the marketplace. His friends are close by, and there are others there to hear him speak. Muhammad welcomes you warmly. He speaks of the greatness of the Jewish people—how they are divinely blessed with wealth and wisdom. He praises your people for being the source of God's prophets.

Curious, you go back to hear him again. This time he is telling a revelation about one of your prophets. Maybe that is a good thing. But wait—this story isn't right. It's different from your Torah, your holy book, which your people have preserved for more than two thousand years. *Who does Muhammad think he is? Does he think we are going to deny our Scriptures and follow him based on talk alone?*

You continue to watch Muhammad closely, and soon you begin to challenge him.

The Jewish people did begin to challenge Muhammad, as we will see in this section.

UNACCEPTABLE CONTRADICTIONS

When Jews went to hear the prophet Muhammad, they discovered that often his new revelations from the angel Gabriel were a repetition of the stories from their Scriptures. Sometimes the stories were almost exactly the same. Other times the story line stayed the same, but the details were changed. Occasionally, completely new stories were presented about biblical characters such as Abraham, Ezra and Jesus.

The Old Testament influence is not a small, insignificant aspect of the Quran. Conservatively estimating, the retelling of Bible stories makes up at least 7 percent of the text.[*] To help you really understand how the stories appear in the Quran, I have included a chart on the following pages listing the major Bible stories told in the order they appear in the Quran.[1]

As you can see from the chart, some stories were told in detail, such as accounts of Joseph and Moses, but most of the descriptions of the prophet's lives were brief. Little bits and pieces were presented here and there. If you only listened to Quranic revelations, it would have been difficult to put together a clear picture about the life of a prophet. The bulk of the information about these people is found in the Jewish and Christian Scriptures.

---

[*] This number is based on the 876 verses referenced in the biblical stories chart compared to the 6,346 verses in the entire Quran.

BIBLE STORIES IN THE QURAN

Quran	Story	Bible
2:35–37	Adam and Eve eat forbidden fruit	Genesis 3:1–6
2:49–50	Jews delivered from Pharaoh	Exodus 12:31–32; 14:21–23
2:51–57	Jews worship calf; God provides manna and quail	Exodus 32:1–5; 16:11–15
2:60	Water out of the rock	Exodus 17:5–6
2:246–247	Israel asks for a king, gets Saul	1 Samuel 8:4–5; 9:27–10:1
2:249–251	Story of Gideon mixed with story of Saul	Judges 7:5–6; 1 Samuel 17
3:38–41	Angel tells Zacharias of the coming birth of John the Baptist	Luke 1:11–17
3:45–49	Angel tells Mary she will give birth to Jesus	Luke 1:26–35
4:1	Mankind created from Adam and Eve	Genesis 1:28; 5
5:27–32	Cain and Abel*	Genesis 4:3–15
7:19–29	Adam and Eve eat forbidden fruit; shame from nakedness; kicked out of the garden	Genesis 3
7:80–84	Lot rescued; evil cities destroyed because of sexual sin	Genesis 19:1–25
7:103–155	Detailed account of Moses in Egypt, including stick turning into snake; the plagues; crossing the sea; the Ten Commandments; Jews asking for an idol to worship; the golden calf and Aaron	Exodus 7–12; 14; 20; 32
10:71–73	Noah and the ark	Genesis 7
10:79–93	Moses and his dealings with Pharaoh in Egypt*	Exodus 7–12
11:25–49	Noah and the Flood*	Genesis 7–8
11:69–82	Abraham visited by angels; Sarah's laugh; Abraham praying on behalf of Lot; angels rescue Lot; evil city destroyed by brimstone	Genesis 18:1–19:29

* This story generally follows the biblical version, but there is additional material as well.

Quran	Story	Bible
12:4–101	Detailed account of Joseph's life, including Joseph's dream; his brothers throwing him into a well; being taken into slavery; his master's wife trying to seduce him; time in prison; interpreting prisoners' dreams; interpreting Pharaoh's dream; being released from prison and promoted; the visit from his brothers	Genesis 37–46
15:51–77	Angels told Abraham that he would have a child and warned that Lot's city would be destroyed; the city destroyed by brimstone	Genesis 18–19
19:2–15	Zacharias and the birth of John the Baptist	Luke 1:11–20, 57–64
19:16–40	Mary and the birth of Jesus*	Luke 1:26–38; 2:1–7
20:9–99	Moses and the burning bush; Moses' staff turning into a snake; Moses' hand becoming leprous; Moses commanded to go to Pharaoh; Aaron is helper; confrontation with Pharaoh's magicians; Moses' snake eats their snakes; Pharaoh's army drowns in the Red Sea; worshiping the golden calf	Exodus 2:1–4:17; 7:8–12; 14; 32
21:51–73	A mixture of the story of Gideon and the story of the three Hebrews in the fiery furnace with Abraham as the main character	Judges 6:28–32; Daniel 3:13–25
21:74–75	Lot saved from the evil city	Genesis 19
21:76–77	Noah and his family spared from the Flood	Genesis 7
21:79–82	Solomon had wisdom*	1 Kings 3:9–11
21:83–84	Job's troubles and restoration	Job 1–2, 42
21:87–88	Jonah punished and rescued	Book of Jonah
21:89–90	Zacharias and the birth of John the Baptist	Luke 1:5–23, 57–66
23:23–44	Noah building the ark; bringing two of each animal on board; people who opposed Noah drowned in the Flood	Genesis 6:13–8:22
23:45–49	Pharaoh denied Moses and Aaron and was destroyed	Exodus 5–14

* This story generally follows the biblical version, but there is additional material as well.

Quran	Story	Bible
26:10–68	Moses and Aaron go to Pharaoh; Moses' stick turns into a snake and eats the snakes of Pharaoh's magicians; parting of the Red Sea; Egyptian army drowns	Exodus 3:10–12; 7:8–12; 14
26:69–104	Abraham rejects his father's idols*	Genesis 12:1–9
26:105–120	Noah was mocked by others, but they were drowned in the Flood as punishment	Genesis 6–7
26:160–175	Lot and the destruction of the evil city; Lot's family saved except for his wife	Genesis 19:1–29
27:7–14	Moses and the burning bush; Moses' stick turns into a snake; Moses' hand becomes leprous	Exodus 3:1–6; 4:1–7
27:54–58	Lot was saved; the evil city was destroyed	Genesis 19:1–29
28:3–40	Moses cast into the river; raised in Pharaoh's house; nursed by his mother; confronted two men fighting and killed one; went to Midian; joined family of shepherds; sees the burning bush; snake and leprosy signs; goes back to Pharaoh; Pharaoh rejects him; God drowns Pharaoh and his army	Exodus 2:1–3:6; 4:1–7; 5:1–12:32; 14
29:14–15	Noah warned the people and was saved on the ark	Genesis 6:9–7:7
29:26–35	Lot preached against sodomy; the evil city destroyed; Lot's family saved*	Genesis 19
30:20	Adam created from dust; Eve created from Adam's rib	Genesis 2:7, 21–22
37:75–83	Noah and the Flood	Genesis 6:9–7:24
37:83–113	Abraham mixed with the story of Gideon; Abraham goes to sacrifice son; angel stops him and provides a ram	Judges 6:28–32; Genesis 22:1–19
37:123–132	Elijah opposes Baal worshipers	1 Kings 18:20–40
37:133–138	Lot and the destruction of the evil city	Genesis 19:1–29
37:139–148	Jonah swallowed by a fish; spit up on land; preached to people; sheltered by a gourd plant	Book of Jonah

* This story generally follows the biblical version, but there is additional material as well.

Bible Stories in the Quran (continued)

Quran	Story	Bible
40:23–54	Moses and Pharaoh; Pharaoh killing the male Hebrew babies; Pharaoh punished*	Exodus 1:15–22; 5–12
43:46–56	Moses gave signs to Pharaoh; Moses couldn't speak well; Egyptians drowned as punishment	Exodus 5–12
44:17–33	Moses and Pharaoh; Israel inherits the wealth of Egypt	Exodus 5–12
51:24–37	Abraham visited by angels; told him a son would be born*	Genesis 18:1–21
51:38–40	Moses and Pharaoh	Exodus 5–12
54:9–16	Noah and the Flood	Genesis 6:13–7:24
54:33–39	Lot and the evil city	Genesis 19:1–29
71:1–28	Noah and the Flood*	Genesis 6:13–7:24
79:15–26	Moses and Pharaoh	Exodus 5–12

* This story generally follows the biblical version, but there is additional material as well.

So you have to make a judgment about Muhammad's revelations. The options are:

A.   Muhammad was telling the truth—he received revelations from the same God who inspired the Scriptures of the Jews and the Christians.

B.   Muhammad repeated these stories after hearing them from the people around him, but he made slight changes due to having a bad memory.

C.   Muhammad was repeating stories he learned from the Bible and adapting them as needed to further his goal to establish Islam in Arabia.

Here's what I believe: The original source for the prophet Muhammad's stories about Abraham and the other prophets is the Bible. I do not think the Quran is a new revelation from the same God who inspired the Bible. One reason is that the Quran and the Bible are often contradictory. I do not think God would choose to give new information that would contradict the record that He had established thousands of years earlier.

The god Muhammad proclaimed does not exist. Muhammad's revelations came from demons. The name *Allah* was used in pre-Islam Arabia to refer to one of the 360 idols in Kaaba. Allah was supposed to be the greatest god. Some tribes used the name to refer to the moon god.

I believe that Muhammad presented stories and principles from Scripture as part of his strategy to win over Jews and Christians. If he built his new religion on the foundation of Judaism and Christianity, he could get more converts.

So why are there differences between the Quran and the Bible? I believe Muhammad introduced differences that he felt would support Islam. I think he truly expected the Jews to accept these changes. They did not.

The Jews Challenge Muhammad

The Jewish community went on the defensive when the Quran began to contradict their Scriptures. They set out to make Muhammad look bad.

One time a Jewish man brought some human bones and laid them in front of Muhammad. "If you are a prophet of God, you can make these bones alive," he said.

Muhammad had no answer, and he couldn't bring the bones back to life. He was embarrassed, and so were the Muslims around him. According to hadith, he even became upset with Allah over this. But Muhammad had a wonderful solution for problems like these—continuing revelation. He announced that the angel Gabriel gave a revelation about this situation. First, the revelation addressed the challenge from the Jewish man.

> So let not their speech, then, grieve you (O Muhammad). Verily, We know what they conceal and what they reveal. Does not man see that We have created him from *Nutfah* (mixed male and female sexual discharge—semen drops). Yet behold he (stands forth) as an open opponent. And he puts forth for Us a parable, and forgets his own creation. He says: "Who will give life to these bones after they are rotten and have become dust?"
>
> —SURAH 36:76–78

Then Allah answered the challenge.

> Say: (O Muhammad) "He will give life to them Who created them for the first time! And He is the All-Knower of every creation!" He Who produces for you fire out of the green tree, when behold you kindle therewith. Is not He Who created the heavens and the earth, Able to create the like of them? Yes, indeed! He is the All-Knowing Supreme Creator. Verily, His Command, when He intends a thing, is only that He says to it, "Be!"—and it is!
>
> —SURAH 36:79–82

In other words, Allah said, "I'm the one who can give bones life, not Muhammad. I can command anything to happen by just saying 'Be.'" However, although Allah claimed the power to do so, he did not revive the dead bones, and the Jews were not impressed with Muhammad's answer.

THE JEWS ASKED FOR A SIGN

The Jewish people frequently asked Muhammad for signs to validate what he was saying. The Quran makes several references to this.

And they say: "Why are not signs sent down to him from his Lord?"

—SURAH 29:50

These words are just like the Jews' words to Jesus six hundred years earlier (recorded in the New Testament).

Then the Jews demanded of him, "What miraculous sign can you show us to prove your authority to do all this?" Jesus answered them, "Destroy this temple, and I will raise it again in three days."*

—JOHN 2:18–19

The Jews sought a sign because of Old Testament prophecies (such as Isaiah 11:1–10 and 25:9).

The Quran answered the challenges for signs several times. One time Allah told Muhammad to answer as follows:

Say: "The signs are only with Allah, and I am only a plain warner." Is it not sufficient for them that We have sent down to you the Book (the Quran) which is recited to them?

—SURAH 29:50–51

In other words, Muhammad was to say to the Jews, "I'm the prophet. Don't ask me for signs. Signs are for Allah to do." And Allah said in the Quran, "The Quran is sign enough for you!"

Another time Allah responded that one sign was the prophecies in the Torah and the Gospel regarding the coming of Muhammad.

They say: "Why does he not bring us a sign (proof) from his Lord?" Has there not come to them the proof of that which is (written) in the former papers [Scriptures,

---

* Jesus' answer was a reference to His body being destroyed by death on the cross and His resurrection three days later.

i.e., the Taurat (Torah), and the Injeel (Gospel), about
the coming of the Prophet Muhammad]?"

—SURAH 20:133

If you are familiar with the Bible, you are probably wondering, *What part prophesies of Muhammad?* If you would like to look at these in detail, please see Appendix C. You will discover that the prophecies claimed by the Muslims often actually refer to Jesus or the Holy Spirit. Islam also teaches that most of the prophecies about Muhammad were taken out of the Bible when the Jews and Christians corrupted their Scriptures. (See chapter fourteen.)

THE JEWS BEGAN TO MOCK MUHAMMAD

Most of the Jews decided Muhammad was not a real prophet. They started to make fun of him and of Islam and the Muslims. The Quran records:

> Indeed, Allah has heard the statement of those (Jews) who say: "Truly, Allah is poor and we are rich!" We shall record what they have said and their killing of the Prophets unjustly, and We shall say: "Taste you the torment of the burning (Fire)."
>
> —SURAH 3:181

> Among those who are Jews, there are some who displace words from (their) right places and say: "We hear your word (O Muhammad) and disobey," and "Hear and let you (O Muhammad) hear nothing." And *Raina* with a twist of their tongues and as a mockery of the religion (Islam).
>
> —SURAH 4:46

The Jews really were making fun of Muhammad, saying, "We hear and *disobey*." They insulted him verbally and in other ways.

A JEWISH WOMAN POISONS THE PROPHET

The Jews in Medina began to see Muhammad as a dangerous threat that needed to be eliminated.[2] The most well-known attempt to kill him was by a Jewish woman who tried to poison him.

I remember from my childhood that our Quran reciter loved to tell this story and embellished it quite a bit to make it exciting. But here I am going to tell the story as it is recorded in Islamic history.

Remember that Muhammad first approached the Jews of Medina with persuasive words. He had friendly relationships with some of them. It would not be unusual for him to eat a meal with them. This story is set in the context of Muhammad eating a meal prepared by a Jewish woman named Zaineb.

Zaineb prepared a lamb on the barbecue. She found out that the prophet liked to eat the shoulder of the lamb the most. So she put extra poison on the shoulder meat, but she poisoned the whole lamb as well.

She brought out the meat and served it to Muhammad and one of his friends. Muhammad took some of the shoulder meat and began to eat it, but he tasted something unusual with the meat. He took it out of his mouth and threw it away. But his friend liked the meat and ate it. He later died from the poison.

Muhammad was furious with Zaineb. He had one of his followers kill her. Muhammad believed that the poison he ate bothered him for the rest of his life. In his last time of sickness, before his death, the sister of the man who died from the poisoned lamb came to visit him. Muhammad told her, "O Ombasheer, what you see in me now [my illness] is the result of my eating from the lamb that I ate with your brother."[3]

Muslims believe that the poison weakened Muhammad's body and caused him to have stomach problems. They can't agree whether the poison really killed him.

To them, this incident is proof that the Jews hated the prophet and were jealous of him and wanted to destroy him. To them it was just one more example of how the Jews opposed the prophets of Allah and how Allah protected Muhammad.

Muslims do not try to see things from the Jewish perspective. They do not consider the fact that after the Jews rejected Islam, they felt threatened by Muhammad and wanted to protect themselves. Muslims just think Jews are thoroughly evil.

CHAPTER 14

The Quran Cancels the Kind Words About the Jews

A FTER ABOUT A YEAR IN MEDINA, Muhammad had only converted a few Jews to Islam. The great majority of them rejected him completely. The Quran comments:

> Allah has cursed them for their disbelief, so they believe not except a few.
> —SURAH 4:46; CF. SURAH 26:196–197

In the next few pages we will see how Muhammad reacted to their rejection. He began receiving more revelations about the Jews, revelations that took away the kind words that were spoken earlier. Let's look specifically at how five kind words of the Quran were reversed. Then we'll look in detail at a major accusation, which was that the Jews changed the words of the Old Testament in order to deny the teachings of Islam.

1. Allah cursed the Jewish people because of their transgressions.

> Those among the Children of Israel who disbelieved were cursed by the tongue of Dawud (David) and Isa (Jesus), son of Maryam (Mary). That was because they disobeyed (Allah and his messengers) and were ever transgressing beyond bounds.
> —SURAH 5:78

The earlier revelation said the Jews were Allah's chosen people (Surah 2:47).

2. Allah transformed Jews into monkeys and pigs as punishment for their wrongdoing.

So when they [the Jews] exceeded the limits of what they were prohibited, We said to them: "Be you monkeys, despised and rejected."

—SURAH 7:166

Shall I inform you of something worse than that, regarding the recompense from Allah: those (Jews) who incurred the Curse of Allah and His Wrath, and those of whom (some) He transformed into monkeys and swines…

—SURAH 5:60

And indeed you knew those amongst you [children of Israel] who transgressed in the matter of the Sabbath (i.e. Saturday). We said to them: "Be you monkeys, despised and rejected."

—SURAH 2:65

Muslims interpret this to mean that Jews were literally turned into animals.[1] But there is no information in the Quran or in the Islamic history to answer the basic questions: 1) When did Allah transform Jews into monkeys and pigs? 2) Where did Allah transform Jews into monkeys and pigs? 3) Did Allah do that to the whole Jewish nation or just some of them? I never found any evidence that something like this happened to the Jewish people during their history.

The earlier revelations spoke of Allah protecting the Jews (in Egypt, for example), not punishing them by turning them into animals.

3. Allah condemns the Jews for killing the prophets.

Why then have you killed the Prophets of Allah afore-time, if you indeed have been believers?

—SURAH 2:91

Verily, We took the covenant of the Children of Israel and sent Messengers to them. Whenever there came to them a Messenger with what they themselves desired not,—a group of them they called liars, and others among them they killed. They thought there would be no *Fitnah* (trial or punishment), so they became blind and deaf...

—SURAH 5:70–71

The earlier revelation praised the Jews for being the source of all Allah's prophets.

4. Islam is the final religion and the Quran is the last testament; therefore, Jews and Christians must convert.

And whoever seeks a religion other than Islam, it will never be accepted of him, and in the Hereafter he will be one of the losers.

—SURAH 3:85

The earlier revelation said that Jews and Christians were only required to believe in God and do good works. They did not have to convert to Islam.

5. The Jewish people corrupted the books of God.

The new revelations accused them of ruining their holy books and taking out the parts that spoke of Muhammad.

A party of them (Jewish rabbis) used to hear the Word of Allah [the Taurat (Torah)], then they used to change it knowingly after they understood it.

—SURAH 2:75; CF. VERSES 76–79

> They [the Jews] change the words from their (right) places and have abandoned a good part of the Message that was sent to them.
>
> —SURAH 5:13

The earlier revelation encouraged Jews and Christians to practice the teachings of their books.

THE CORRUPTION OF THE SCRIPTURES

I need to make a few extra comments about the corruption of Scriptures. This belief in Islam is very important because it explains for Muslims why the Bible says so little about Muhammad and also why there are contradictions between the Bible and the Quran.

The corruption of Scripture raises a lot of questions. Where are the original, uncorrupted copies? Muslims say, "They disappeared." They have nothing to show what the original books said. They cannot say when the corruption happened—just that it was long before the days of Muhammad. They can't say who did it or what was changed. There is no proof at all.

Muslim scholars theorize that Christians took out the parts of the New Testament that prophesied Muhammad would come. They say that Christians added in parts about the Trinity, Jesus being God's son, Jesus dying on the cross and salvation by the blood of Jesus.

For the Old Testament, they say the Jews took out the parts that hurt the reputation of Jews, especially parts about them killing the prophets and being turned into monkeys and pigs as punishment. Muslim scholars also say that the differences between stories in the Quran and the Old Testament were due to the Jews changing their Scriptures.

Muslim scholars say there are still a few verses left in the Old and New Testaments that speak of the final prophet,

Muhammad. I heard about these verses when I was a Muslim, but I never looked at a Bible to read them in context. Only those who specialized in Quranic commentary would do that. (My major was Islamic culture and history.) If you are interested in seeing these verses, you can refer to Appendix C. People who understand Judaism or Christianity will immediately recognize that Muslim scholars misinterpret these verses.

CONCLUSION

In this chapter you have seen how the good words about the Jews were canceled. You also learned about the key Muslim claim that Jews and Christians corrupted the Bible, which made it necessary for Allah to send the Quran. In the next chapter you will see how the Quran continued to expand the case against the Jews.

CHAPTER 15

Expanding the Case Against the Jews

MUHAMMAD HAD DECIDED THE JEWS WERE his enemy, and the new Quranic revelations were providing plenty of evidence against them. The following verses from the Quran are the foundation of much of the hatred in the Islamic world toward Jews.

1. The Quran says that the Jews are the greatest enemies of Islam.

> Verily, you will find the strongest among men in enmity to the believers (Muslims) the Jews and those who are Al-Mushrikun [idolaters, polytheists, disbelievers in the Oneness of Allah, pagans]...
>
> —SURAH 5:82

This verse speaks of both Jews and idol worshipers; however, the idol worshipers did not prove to be much of a threat to Muhammad because they quickly converted to Islam. Therefore, Jews were known as the number one enemy of Islam because they continued to resist being converted.

2. The Quran says that Jewish people do not love Muslims and will not love a Muslim until he converts to Judaism.

> Never will the Jews nor the Christians be pleased with you (O Muhammad) till you follow their religion.
>
> —SURAH 2:120

3. The Quran says that Jews start wars and cause trouble in the earth.

> We have put enmity and hatred amongst them [the Jews] till the Day of Resurrection. Every time they kindled the fire of war, Allah extinguished it; and they (ever) strive to make mischief on the earth.
>
> —SURAH 5:64; CF. VERSE 67

This idea that Jews are behind all wars is espoused throughout the Islamic world. One example is this excerpt from the covenant of Hamas, the Islamic jihad group that sponsors many suicide bombings in Israel.

> They [the Jews] stood behind World War I...and formed the League of Nations through which they could rule the world. They were behind World War II, through which they made huge financial gains...There is no war going on anywhere without them having their finger in it.
>
> —ARTICLE 22 FROM THE COVENANT OF HAMAS[1]

4. The Quran condemns both Jews and Christians for saying Allah has a son. The Quran claims that Jews call Ezra the son of God (which they don't).

> And the Jews say: 'Uzair (Ezra) is the son of Allah, and the Christians say: Messiah is the son of Allah. That is their saying with their mouths, resembling the saying of those who disbelieved aforetime. Allah's Curse be on them, how they are deluded away from the truth!
>
> —SURAH 9:30; CF. 5:73; 4:159

5. The Quran condemns Jews and Christians for saying they are children of God. In Islam it is blasphemy to say, "I am a child of God."

> And (both) the Jews and the Christians say: "We are the

children of Allah and His loved ones." Say: "Why then does He punish you for your sins?" Nay, you are but human beings of those He has created...

—SURAH 5:18

6. The Quran says the Jews are cursed because they accused Allah of having a weak hand.

The Jews say: "Allah's hand is tied up (i.e. He does not give and spend of His Bounty)." Be their hands tied up and be they accursed for what they uttered.

—SURAH 5:64

7. The Quran says that Jews love the present life of this world and do not care about things of eternity.

And verily, you will find them (the Jews) the greediest of mankind for life...Everyone of them wishes he could be given a life of a thousand years. But the grant of such life will not save him even a little from (due) punishment.

—SURAH 2:96

From the Islamic point of view, one of the worst things a person can do is to forget eternity and focus on this present life.

8. The Quran says that Jewish people claim to have killed the Messiah.

This accusation really doesn't make any sense. The Jews didn't even believe the Messiah had come, so they certainly were not telling people that they had killed him.

And because of their [the Jews] saying (in boast), "We killed Messiah 'Isa (Jesus), son of Maryam (Mary), the Messenger of Allah,"—but they killed him not, nor crucified him, but it appeared so to them [the resemblance of 'Isa (Jesus) was put over another man (and they killed that man)]...

—SURAH 4:157

This verse points to the corruption and lack of sensibility in the Quran. This verse is a lie against both the Jews and Christians. It presents a false picture that the Jews accepted Jesus as Messiah, and it denies that the real Jesus was crucified.

CONCLUSION

According to the above points, the Quran concluded that the Jewish people were no longer the chosen people of Allah (Surah 3:110). The followers of Islam were now the chosen people who had the job of protecting the one true religion.

The Quran's statements about the Jews became increasingly aggressive and hostile. In the next chapter, you will see that the revelations finally led up to Muhammad declaring war on all the Jews of Arabia.

CHAPTER **16**

Muhammad Prepares to Drive the Jews Out of Arabia

THE RELATIONSHIP BETWEEN MUHAMMAD AND THE Jews is like a relationship between two friends that went sour. One of the friends is affected so much that he becomes obsessed, saying bad things about his old friend and forgetting the good things he said earlier.

In my opinion, if the Christians and Jews of Mecca or Medina had converted to Islam, there never would have been holy war. If the Christians and Jews had accepted Muhammad's revelations, then Muhammad would have continued to use the strategy of persuasive preaching. But their rejection made Muhammad feel that he was surrounded by his enemies and needed to protect himself and his revelation of Islam. At first he gathered power as a means of self-defense, but later its purpose was to force submission from those who rejected his message.

REJECTING THE JEWS

As Muhammad's frustration grew with the rejection from the Jews of Medina, he received a revelation that warned Muslims not to be friends with Jews.

> O you who believe! Take not as friends the people who incurred the Wrath of Allah (i.e. the Jews). Surely, they

have despaired of (receiving any good in) the Hereafter.

—SURAH 60:13

Previously, Muhammad instructed his followers to face Jerusalem to pray. In January 624 he changed direction to face Mecca. The Quran comments:

And from wheresoever you start forth (for prayers), turn your face in the direction of *Al-Masjid-Al-Haram* (at Makkah), that is indeed the truth from your Lord. And Allah is not unaware of what you do.

—SURAH 2:149

These words directed Muslims to face the sacred mosque in Mecca, where the Kaaba was located.

THREATENING THE JEWS

As Muhammad's frustration grew, he started making severe threats to Jews and Christians in an attempt to get them to convert. Here is an example of one of those threats.

O you who have been given the Scripture (Jews and Christians)! Believe in what We have revealed (to Muhammad) confirming what is (already) with you, before We efface faces (by making them like the back of necks; without nose, mouth, eyes) and turn them hindwards, or curse them as We cursed the Sabbath-breakers. And the commandment of Allah is always executed.

—SURAH 4:47

DECLARING THE VERSE OF THE SWORD

Finally, Muhammad declared he had received new revelations that showed the final picture of the relationship between Islam and those who do not accept Islam, especially the Jews and the Christians.[1] At that time, the world started to hear a revelation called *the verse of the sword.*

> Kill the *Mushrikun* [unbelievers] wherever you find them, and capture them and besiege them, and lie in wait for them in each and every ambush. But if they repent and perform *As-Salat (Iqamat-as-Salat)* [the five ritual prayers per day], and give *Zakat* [alms], then leave their way free. Verily, Allah is Oft-Forgiving, Most Merciful.
>
> —SURAH 9:5

This verse commanded Muslims to go before every single Jewish person (as well as every other kind of unbeliever) on earth and to submit him to Islam. Submission meant he must convert and accept Muhammad as the prophet of Allah or pay a tax for remaining in his faith. If he refused, the sword would cut his neck.

From Islamic history we know that this verse focuses particularly on Jews and Christians. That's because after Muhammad's successful invasion of Mecca, most of the idol worshipers had already accepted Islam. The idol worshipers didn't feel that their idols were worth dying for. However, the Jews and Christians were still clinging to their faiths. Keep in mind that the Christians were a small group, not even practicing a pure form of Christianity. So they were not very important to Muhammad. But the Jews—they were the ones that he wanted to subdue. They had a lot of wealth, they were openly resisting his preaching, and they were trying to partner with Muhammad's enemies.

After the verse of the sword, it was now the duty of Muslims to kill those who refused to believe in Islam or to pay the tax. The wealthy Jews paid the tax and continued to practice Judaism. Some of the poorer Jews could not pay the tax, but they refused to accept Islam. They were killed.

ALLAH WILL FIGHT AGAINST THE JEWS

The Quran says that Allah would use the Muslims to punish

the Jews. Muslims would experience healing in their hearts from serving Allah this way.

> Fight against them so that Allah will punish them by your hands and disgrace them and give you victory over them and heal the breasts of a believing people, and remove the anger of their (believers') hearts. Allah accepts the repentance of whom He wills. Allah is All-Knowing, All-Wise.
>
> —SURAH 9:14–15

In modern times, we have seen Muslims experience this kind of satisfaction from fighting Israel and her allies. Palestinians and other Muslims in the Middle East were dancing with joy in the streets after the events of September 11, 2001. They receive peace and satisfaction from the deaths of people who support Israel. The attacks temporarily relieved the anger in the Muslims' hearts over the existence of the modern state of Israel.

ALL RELIGIONS OTHER THAN ISLAM MUST BE DESTROYED

The final revelations of the Quran commanded Muslims to destroy any form of religion that was not submitted to Allah. It became their duty to go and kill Jews, Christians and any other non-Muslims. The goal was to make Islam the only religion controlling the world.

> And fight them until there is no more *Fitnah* (disbelief and polytheism, i.e. worshiping others besides Allah) and the religion (worship) will be for Allah Alone [in the whole of the world]. But if they cease (worshiping others besides Allah), then certainly, Allah is All-Seer of what they do.
>
> —SURAH 8:39

The only way to stop being the object of attack is to stop worshiping other gods besides Allah.

CONCLUSION

In the past four chapters you saw progressive revelation (*nasikh*) in action. At first, Muhammad's revelations were favorable toward Jews. Then the revelations began to cancel out the favorable words. Finally the revelations called for Muslims to reject the Jews and to convert them by the sword.

These were not just idle words. Let's see what Muhammad did personally to the Jewish tribes in his area.

CHAPTER 17

The Arabian Holocaust

THERE WERE THREE MAJOR JEWISH TRIBES in Medina, and they all suffered at the hands of the prophet of Islam. I can *tell* you that what happened to the Jews was bad, but I want to *show* you it was bad. I want you to know exactly what Muhammad did and recorded for Islamic history.

This chapter will cover three major events:

* The revenge Muhammad took on a Jewish village where someone tried to assassinate him (the Nadir tribe, 625)

* The slaughter of hundreds from a Jewish tribe that assisted Mecca in an unsuccessful attack against Muhammad (the Qurayzah tribe, 627)

* The conquest of the Jews who had fled to the nearby village of Khaybar (628)[1]

May I remind you of something here? You are about to read about the actions of Muhammad. This is the founder of Islam. This is not somebody who is reinterpreting the holy books of Islam years after they were written. He is the one who received the revelation. He is the one who is the best Muslim. Look at the example that Muhammad set!

SETTING THE STAGE

To understand the situation, it helps to know about

107

Muhammad's battles up to this point.

After he left Mecca, no one from Mecca followed him or harmed him. They let him go. But Muhammad went to ambush one of the Meccan caravans returning from Syria. This attack was more than just damage to their business; it was an attack against their survival. The caravans went out only twice a year. They returned with food, sugar, salt and clothing that the people needed to survive. Mecca was in a desert where they couldn't produce very much food, so they really depended on trade. If Muhammad had succeeded in his attack on the caravan, Mecca would have suffered from many shortages.

As it was, the Meccan caravan heard about Muhammad's plot and avoided the place where he was waiting in ambush. The people of Mecca decided, however, that Muhammad needed to be punished for his actions. They went to fight him, and the two parties met in the valley of Badr. Muhammad and his forces won a surprise victory (Battle of Badr, 624). This made him the strongest leader in Arabia.

DESTROYING THE DATE PALMS OF THE NADIR TRIBE (625)

Muhammad was not always hostile to this Jewish tribe. He was friendly with some of the people of the Nadir ["NAY deer"] tribe and sometimes visited their homes. Islamic history says that one time a Jewish man went up to the house Muhammad was visiting and tried to throw a rock at Muhammad to kill him.

Muhammad wasn't hurt, but Muhammad said he received a revelation about what that man was trying to do, so he left the village and went back to Medina. He told the Muslim people what happened. A few days later Muhammad commanded his people to prepare for jihad and the conquest of the Nadir tribe.[2]

Muhammad and his military put the village under siege for six nights to force the villagers to come out. The Jewish villagers were prepared to fight, and they had built bunkers all around the city.[3] Instead of fighting them, Muhammad instructed his soldiers to cut down all of the palm trees around the village and burn them.

These trees weren't just for looks. They were date palms, the source of livelihood for this tribe.[4] The Jewish people in the village shouted, "O Muhammad, you had prohibited people to burn trees in a village. Why do you do this to us?"[5]

Some of the Muslim soldiers weren't happy that Muhammad forced them to destroy the date palms. But the Jewish people surrendered and asked Muhammad to let them leave the village with their basic necessities—cows, camels, food and clothing. Muhammad agreed to this, but he did not allow them to take their weapons.

When the people left their village, according to Islamic history, the women and children were singing and clapping and reciting psalms.[6] The Jews wanted to let Muhammad and his people know that they stood behind their God—the God of Abraham, Isaac and Jacob—and they were not going to give up their faith. The people went to another Jewish village to the north of Medina called Khaybar.

Muhammad confiscated all the villagers' money and divided it amongst his soldiers.[7]

Later, Muhammad told his people that Allah was rejoicing in heaven over what he did to the Jewish people. Allah sent a Quranic chapter to Muhammad about this event. This is Surah 59, called "The Gathering." It mentions many details, including the destruction of the palm trees, the Jews going into exile and distribution of the booty.

MASSACRE OF THE MEN OF
THE QURAYZAH TRIBE (627)

After what happened to the Nadir tribe, the people of the Qurayzah ["Kor RAY zuh"] tribe, who were still living in the area, recognized that Muhammad was a threat to their lives, if not today, then tomorrow. In defense of their future, they decided to work together with the people of Mecca to try to overthrow Muhammad.

Muhammad heard about the impending attack and asked one of his friends for advice. This friend suggested that Muhammad dig a trench all around Medina, which he did. When the Meccan army came, they could not get past the trench. They shot arrows at Medina, and Muhammad's forces shot arrows back. It was actually a very light battle. After a while, the Meccan army decided that it could not get past the trench, and it retreated.

ALLAH CALLS FOR REVENGE

After this battle, Muhammad said that the angel Gabriel came one afternoon to him in the form of a man wearing a head cover and riding a mule. Gabriel asked, "Did you leave your weapon behind [at the Battle of the Trench]? Why don't you get your sword and the jihad will continue… The angels of Allah never put their swords away. They are always ready to join you. Allah has commanded you to go to the children of Qurayzah, and I am going before you to them and I will shake the village."

It was almost time for the third prayer of the day. Muhammad went to the mosque and announced, "No one is going to do the third prayer here [in Medina]. We are going to do it in the village of the Qurayzah tribe." All Muslims understood this to mean they would go that day to attack the Qurayzah.[8]

Muhammad believed that Allah would help him defeat this last Jewish tribe. After they arrived at the village, Muhammad asked his soldiers, "Did you see anyone walking in front of you on the way here?"

They replied, "Yes, a man named De-hayah Al-Kalbi. He was riding a mule." This was a real person living in Medina that everyone recognized.

Muhammad responded, "This is the angel Gabriel who came in the form of this man to shake the Jewish village and put fear in the hearts of the Jewish people."[9]

THE JEWS SURRENDER AND ARE SLAUGHTERED

Muhammad and his military put the village under siege for twenty-five days. The Jews were tired and afraid that Muhammad would kill them all. They realized that he would not leave until they surrendered, so they asked to surrender under the same terms as the people of Nadir, who were permitted to leave their village and take along the necessities of life.

However, after the Jews surrendered, Muhammad asked the leader of the pagan converts in Medina what he should do with the Jewish people. This man answered, "My judgment is to kill the men and divide the money, women and children among the soldiers."

Muhammad agreed and told his friend, "You judged them with the judgment of Allah."[10]

Muhammad went to Medina's marketplace and commanded his people to dig trenches. Then they told all the Jewish men to march into these trenches.

As they were going, the Jewish people said to the leader of their tribe, "Look at what Muhammad is doing to us. Where do you think they are going to take us, and what do you think they are going to do to us?"

Their leader replied, "He is taking us to our deaths."

Indeed he was. Muhammad and his people killed between eight hundred and nine hundred Jewish men that day.[11] Their form of death was to cut the men's necks with swords and let them bleed to death quickly. Then they buried the bodies in the trenches. The first part of the advice from Muhammad's friend had been accomplished. Now they turned to the second part.

WOMEN AND CHILDREN SOLD AS SLAVES

The prophet Muhammad took the money, women and children. First he kept 20 percent for himself. Then he divided the rest among his soldiers. Islamic history records that a soldier without a horse got one share. A soldier with a horse got three shares.[12] The record also describes how one man used his share of the spoils. He took the money, women and children that he received to a nearby city to exchange them for horses and swords. The Jewish women and children were merely property that was sold to buy more tools of war.

LESSONS LEARNED

What can we see from this piece of the history between Muhammad and the Jews?

* Muhammad attacked first. After he went to Medina, the people of Mecca left him alone. Muhammad started the battles and retaliations when he ambushed Mecca's caravan.

* The Jews were acting in self-defense. They were not trying to take money, land or houses from anybody else. They were just trying to protect what they had.

* Muhammad believed Allah was helping him in his attack against the Jews.

After the attacks you have just read about, there were only a few Jews remaining in the area, who were living in the village of Khaybar ["KAY bar"], where they had gone after being expelled from Medina earlier. Muhammad turned his attention to them the following year.

DRIVING JEWS OUT OF THE VILLAGE OF KHAYBAR (628)

Muhammad and his military arrived at Khaybar in the nighttime, and he commanded his people to lay siege to the village. That night he told his army, "Tomorrow morning I will give the authority to command the military in this battle to one who loves Allah and his messenger, and Allah and his messenger love him." Everyone was hoping to be the one Muhammad would call. The next morning Muhammad chose Ali ibn Talib, his cousin, and gave him the banner of war to carry into battle.

Early in the morning some Jewish farmers went out to go to their farms, and they saw Muhammad and his military surrounding the city. They started shouting, "Muhammad and his army! Muhammad and his army!" to warn their people.

When Muhammad heard them, he declared, "*Allah o akbar*! [God is great.] Khaybar was destroyed when we entered the land. This will be a dark morning for the people of this land."[13]

The Jewish people who were able to fight took up swords and ran out of their houses to defend their village. The most powerful fighter in the village went to Ali and stood before him. He challenged Ali to fight him one on one.

There was a tradition that when two armies met, they could choose not to fight one army against the other. Instead, each side could send their greatest hero, and they would fight each other. Whichever hero won would declare his side the winner. This is like what happened with David and Goliath in the Bible.

Ali and the Jewish man fought, and Ali prevailed and killed him. This was the sign that Khaybar could not defend itself anymore. The Muslim military attacked the village, and it surrendered.

The Muslims took a large spoil from Khaybar. They were rejoicing and celebrating, saying, "O victor, O victor, kill and kill."

Choosing a Jewish Slave

After Khaybar surrendered, the prophet Muhammad took two young Jewish ladies and walked with them one at a time in front of the bodies of the dead Jewish people. The first girl covered her eyes and face and started crying. She took the dust from the ground and threw it on her face in anguish. When Muhammad saw her doing that, he shouted to his soldiers, "Take this satanic woman away." Then he walked with the second girl, whose name was Sophia. She kept silent. Muhammad put his robe around her as a sign to his soldiers that he would take her to be his own slave.[14]

Muhammad's Zero Tolerance for Judaism

At the end of the battle against Khaybar, Muhammad took the spoil and divided it among his soldiers. Then he stood and made a very important statement to them. He declared, "There will never be two religions in Arabia."[15]

Muslims have been faithful to practice this statement until the present day. Nobody will see another religion or faith that can challenge Islam in Arabia. You will never see a Jewish synagogue anywhere in Saudi Arabia. This happened fourteen hundred years ago, but the picture is the same until today. There is no Jewish life in Saudi Arabia. This shows how close the Saudi Arabians are to Islamic law and practicing the word of Muhammad.

Not more than one year later, Muhammad made another significant statement about the Jews during a sermon at his mosque. He declared that he would continue to destroy the Jewish community in Arabia and that he would clean the land from the evil of Jews and Judaism.[16]

Muhammad and the Muslims successfully reached his goal. The Jewish community disappeared from Arabia as a result of the Muslims killing them, converting some of them and selling them as slaves in the markets. There were no longer two religions in Arabia, just as Muhammad had declared.

FIGHTING THE JEWS UNTIL THE DAY OF JUDGMENT

The Quran and Muhammad taught Muslims very specifically that their battle with Jews would never end.

Karen Armstrong, a popular religious scholar, says that Muhammad didn't have "any hostility towards Jews in general, but only towards the three rebel tribes."[17] This statement is incorrect, because in hadith we can read Muhammad's own opinion.

Muhammad taught that the Muslims would fight the Jews until the Day of Resurrection. By this time, Muslims would have killed all the Jews but one. This one Jew would hide behind a rock, and the rock would say to the Muslims, "There is a Jew hiding behind me. Come and kill him."[18] Muhammad did not expect Judgment Day to come in his lifetime, but he expected it sometime in the near future. In reference to Judgment Day, the Quran says the "Hour has drawn near" (Surah 54:1). So, until the Day of Resurrection comes, committed Muslims are fighting an "unfinished battle" against the Jews.

GIVING MUSLIMS INCENTIVES TO FIGHT

We know Muhammad carried a great grudge against the Jews, but did his followers share his angst? In my opinion, Muhammad's followers didn't have a deep hatred in their hearts toward the Jews. They were just motivated by Muhammad's teachings about jihad.

First of all, Muhammad promised they would get a portion of the spoils from any victory. The Jews offered rich spoils if conquered.

However, money alone was not sufficient motivation, as became evident when Muhammad's army lost the Battle of Uhud against the Meccans (625). Many Muslim soldiers ran away during this war to avoid being killed.

Muhammad needed a way to keep them from running away. He developed a new strategy to deal with this situation. This strategy had two parts. The first part was to inform his soldiers that they would burn in hell if they ran away (Surah 9:38–39, 41). The second part was to let them know that if they did die in battle, they would immediately enter Paradise, have seventy virgins awaiting them and have all the alcohol they wanted to drink (Surah 9:20–21; 55:56, 72; 47:15).[19]

There is a whole chapter in the Quran that describes what Allah was preparing in Paradise for Muslims, especially the ones who were killed in a holy war (jihad). (See Surah 55, titled Most Gracious, especially verses 72, 74 and 76.)

Muslims were also taught that when a Muslim was killed in jihad, two women from heaven would wipe the dust from his face and tell him, "Allah will put this dust on the face of your killer, and he will kill your killer."[20] In other words Allah promised to take revenge on anyone who killed a Muslim who was fighting jihad.

With these motivations, the Muslims were willing to fight and kill their Jewish neighbors as well as any other resident of Arabia who refused to submit to Islam. These motivations are still effective today.

SECTION 5

PHASE THREE OF THE UNFINISHED BATTLE: THE JEWS SCATTERED AND SUBDUED (632–1898)

CHAPTER 18

Muslims Continue Muhammad's Legacy

MUHAMMAD WRECKED THE LIFE OF JEWS in Arabia. He forced them to leave Arabia just as Titus forced them out of Rome. Even after the Jews spread out to different countries, Islam followed them. Again and again, they were trapped under the authority of Islam.

When the Islamic military ruled a country, Islamic law automatically became the standard. According to Islamic law, Jews and Christians had three choices: convert to Islam, pay the tax to the Muslim authority and remain in their faith, or be killed. (The idol worshipers didn't even have the option of paying tax. They only had two options: accept Islam or be killed.)

During the rule of Umar ibn al-Khattab, the picture of the way Muslims should treat Jews and Christians, known as "People of the Book," was finalized.* Remember that Umar walked and talked with Muhammad. Umar was the source of many hadith, and he gave his daughter Hafsa to Muhammad as a wife. Umar came to power only four years after Muhammad's death.

The point is that Umar was close to the prophet, and he ruled the Islamic empire the way Muhammad would have

---

* Samaritans were also considered People of the Book because they were practicing parts of Judaism.

wanted. That's why these guidelines are significant—they are close to the source.

These guidelines were meant to be followed by Muslims and Muslim authority at that time and in the future. I will present to you a list of these guidelines, which I have organized by subject.

GUIDELINES FOR PEOPLE OF THE BOOK

Showing deference to Muslims

* People of the Book were not permitted to show any disrespect toward Muslims or animosity toward Islam, the prophet himself or the Quran.

* If a Jew or Christian were sitting by the road and a Muslim walked by, the Jew or Christian must stand in respect to the Muslim.

* If a Jew or Christian were walking on the road, and he met a Muslim coming from the other direction, the Jew or Christian must turn around and find another road to walk through.

* People of the Book were not permitted to ride horses. They had to ride donkeys, and the Muslims could ride horses.

* People of the Book were required to ride their donkeys sidesaddle (not with one leg on each side of the animal as the Muslims did on their horses).

* People of the Book were not allowed to build their houses higher than the Muslim houses. (The height of the house was important because it was a symbol of honor. Muslims were always supposed to be above non-Muslims.)

* A Jewish or Christian man was not permitted to marry a Muslim woman. However, a Muslim

man could marry a Christian or Jewish woman if he chose to do so.

Not offending Muslims

* People of the Book were not allowed to drink alcohol in front of Muslims. They could drink alcohol in their houses, but they could not appear drunk outside their houses where Muslims could see them.

* Christians were not allowed to let Muslims see the pigs that they were raising. The pigs had to stay hidden.

* Christians and Jews were not allowed to bury their dead during the daylight where a Muslim might see. They had to take the casket quietly at night to the cemetery and bury it. They were not permitted to cry for their dead in public where a Muslim might see or hear them.

Practicing their religion

* In the Jewish synagogues or Christian churches, people were not allowed to raise their voices loud enough to be heard outside the building.

* The Muslims did not want to see or hear People of the Book practicing their religion or their holy days. People of the Book could not celebrate in public.

* People of the Book were not allowed to try to convert Muslims away from Islam.

Law, government, military

* People of the Book were prohibited from holding high positions in the Islamic government.

* People of the Book were prohibited from serving in the Islamic military.

* People of the Book were not allowed to help anyone declaring war against Muslims.

* People of the Book were not permitted to carry weapons.

* People of the Book could not testify against a Muslim in court.

* A Muslim could not be killed because of a Christian or Jew. In other words, if a Muslim killed a Jew, he could not be punished by death for that crime. (Muhammad said in hadith, "A Muslim believer cannot be killed for an infidel.")

Special clothing

* People of the Book had to wear special clothing and special colors that identified them as non-Muslims. Christians wore blue; Jews wore yellow; Samaritans wore red. Both men and women wore these colors.

* Christian women had to wear a sash around their waists.

* Christian and Jewish women had to wear shoes of different colors. In other words, the left shoe had to be a different color than the right shoe. They had to wear shoes that didn't match!

* Christians were not permitted to enter any public place without wearing a large cross around their necks. It had to be made of metal, and it needed to be heavy enough to be uncomfortable, probably about two pounds.[1]

The attitude behind these rules is that People of the Book were impure, filthy infidels, like a disease. Muslims should not have contact with them. Muslims should never appear to be lower than the Jews.

Leaders among Christians and Jews were responsible for enforcing these rules. If these guidelines were violated, the guilty party would be taken to Islamic court and punishment would be decided there.

MY STUDENTS' REACTIONS

When I taught Islamic history in Egypt, I presented this information to my students. They were very comfortable with the guidelines for ruling non-Muslims. They liked to see Muhammad's successors stand up for Islam against the infidels. Most students complained, "Look how far we have fallen. The Christians in Egypt are not following these rules. Our Muslim leader is not strong enough to stand up for Islam." They longed for the past to be real in the present.

THE GUIDELINES IN PRACTICE

Umar, the second leader of the Islamic world, enforced these guidelines. Any leader after him who was following Islam faithfully would adhere to these guidelines. When leaders were not faithful to the guidelines, the Muslims themselves sometimes took matters into their own hands. For example:

* An angry mob of Arabs in Spain killed five thousand Jews because they felt the Jews had too much political power (1066).[2]

* Arab mobs killed thousands of Jews throughout Morocco (1465). In the city of Fez, only eleven Jews were left alive. The attacks were started by

reports of a Jewish man treating a Muslim woman in an offensive manner.[3]

These are just two examples. Many more examples of mass murders, destruction of synagogues and forced conversion to Islam could be given.[4]

Some of the worst persecution of Jews at the hands of Muslim authorities occurred in Egypt from 996 to 1301. At this time, Egypt was the seat of authority in the Islamic world.

Starting in 1006, the Muslim leader of Egypt (Sultan Al-Hakim Beamur-Allah) gave the Jews and Christians two options: accept Islam or leave Egypt. Millions of Christians converted to Islam. This Egyptian leader took all the money and property belonging to the remaining Christians and Jews.

He went to the Jewish community in Cairo and burned down the entire neighborhood—the houses, shops, synagogues, everything. Next he took all the Jews that were left and banished them to an area south of Cairo.[5]

SOME TOLERANCE

This discussion would be incomplete without mentioning that some Muslims became tolerant of Jews and Christians. They accepted Jews and benefited from their talents. For example:

* Muawiya (661–680), the first caliph who was not an associate of Muhammad, was tolerant toward Jews and considered them to be his "faithful allies."[6]

* Jewish bankers were influential in Muslim Baghdad (c. 880–930).[7]

* In Spain the Muslim authority was split into small principalities, and Jewish dignitaries were permitted positions of high authority (1031).[8]

But it is important to remember that the Muslims who behaved this way were going *against* the teachings of their book and the example of their prophet.

THE CRUSADES CAUSE BACKLASH AGAINST JEWS

The relationship between Muslims, Jews and Christians sank to a new low with the start of the Crusades in 1099.

The first Crusade succeeded in taking over Jerusalem. The city surrendered, and thousands of Muslims took refuge in and around the Al-Aqsa Mosque (built on the Temple Mount), where the Crusader army attacked and killed them. Muslim historians say that when the soldiers rode their horses through the mosque, the blood on the ground was so deep that it covered the horses' hooves.

Muslims believed the purpose of the Crusades was to convert them to Christianity because the Quran told them:

> Never will the Jews nor the Christians be pleased with you (O Muhammad) till you follow their religion.
> —SURAH 2:120

The Roman Catholic Church was behind the Crusades, and church leaders stated that their purpose was to liberate the Holy Land and Jerusalem from Muslims. In reality, a lot of the motivation was economic. The European economy was in trouble, and the East appeared to offer a source of wealth.

Crusaders were Christians from Europe, but their attack caused Muslims to increase their distrust of Jews and the Christians in the Middle East.[9]

During the ten crusades that occurred, the Muslims turned back to the Quran and looked at the verse that said Christians and Jews are your greatest enemy (Surah 5:82).[10] They renewed their hostility toward both Christians and Jews. But what did the Jews have to do with the Crusades?

Nothing! The Jews did not cause the Crusades. But, from the Quran, Muslims believed that the enemies of Islam would stand together and fight—even Christians and Jews would fight together.

> O you who believe! take not the Jews and the Christians for your friends and protectors: they are but friends and protectors to each other.
> —SURAH 5:51, ALI TRANSLATION

This was really a misunderstanding of the relationship between Christians and Jews; nevertheless, this is what the Muslims believed. As a result, they increased their persecution against the Jews living among them in fear that they would join the attacks by the Christians.

The Crusades made a lasting impact on the Muslim psyche. For example, when Osama bin Laden and his partners wrote their *fatwa** against Israel and the United States, they titled it "Jihad Against Jews and Crusaders." This document, written in 1998, complained about the "the crusader-Zionist alliance."[11]

THE COLONIAL ERA

In the last one hundred years, the biggest impact on the Muslim psyche came from Western colonialism in the Middle East.

In World War I, the Islamic Turkish Empire sided with the Central Powers of Germany and Austria-Hungary. After the Allied Forces (Great Britain, France, Russia, Serbia and eventually the United States) won the war, the Turkish Empire was dismantled. Nations such as Great Britain, France and Italy took control of land and benefited from new natural resources, more markets for their products and a new place

---

* A legal opinion or decree handed down by an Islamic religious leader.

for their people to colonize. From the Muslim point of view, the colonial powers stole the wealth of their land and attacked their way of life.

The colonial takeover reminded the Muslims of the Crusades. It reinforced their bad attitude toward Christians and Jews. At Al-Azhar University I taught my students that the weakness of the Muslim countries was the fault of the conquest by the Western colonial powers and the lack of Islam in their lives. I told them, "We lost our freedom. We became a target for Christians and Jews to destroy because we are far away from the ways of Umar. All we have today are weak and evil Muslim leaders who are puppets of the Christians and Jews. Their evil laws and culture have ruined our society."

CHRISTIANS ARE NOT INNOCENT

Let me acknowledge here that when it comes to persecuting people of different faiths, Christians are also guilty. Many times they treated Jews and Muslims very badly during their history. (I could list many horrible things, including the Holocaust of World War II.) In fact, when someone brings up these parts of their history, Christians don't know what to say.

It is very important that people understand that there is a major difference between the bad behavior of Muslims and the bad behavior of Christians. The next chapter will explain this difference.

CHAPTER 19

Comparing Islamic Holy War and the Crusades

I WAS AT A PRAYER MEETING ON a military base when a distinguished gentleman stood up and asked me a question I've heard many times: "You talk about the bloody history of the Muslims, but what about the blood on the hands of the Christians? What about the Crusades?"

This is a good question, and I believe every Christian should be able to answer it with confidence.

On the surface, Christians and Muslims both appear to be killing in the name of God. So what's the difference? You have to look at the source of their beliefs:

* What do their books say?
* Whose example are they following?

WHAT DO THE BOOKS SAY?

We cannot judge Islam by what Muslims do, and we cannot judge Christianity by what Christians do. We judge Islam by what the Quran teaches, just as we must judge Christianity by what the New Testament teaches.

You will not find one word in the Gospels where Jesus commanded Christians to kill in the name of Christianity. Not one time did Jesus ever fight His enemies. A Christian who claims to be shedding blood in the name of Christianity is not following the teachings of Jesus. The Crusades and the

131

Holocaust are a sad statement on how far some Christians strayed from the teachings of the New Testament.

On the other hand, you will find holy war everywhere in the Quran. The Quran teaches how, when, where and why Muslims must fight. When Muslims fight in the name of Allah, they are obeying the literal teachings of the Quran.

WHOSE EXAMPLE ARE THEY FOLLOWING?

The example of Muhammad and his friends

After he migrated to Medina, Muhammad became a military leader. He personally led twenty-seven battles against his enemies. He placed great value on Muslims who went to battle with him and fought vigorously (Surah 4:95).

The leaders of Islam followed his example. After Muhammad died, many people who had converted to Islam by force imagined freedom. They thought that Islamic leadership would be distracted with trying to establish a new authority, so they began to abandon Islam. However, Abu Bakr ["BAW ker"], one of Muhammad's closest friends, was quickly recognized as successor. He spent the first three months of his authority killing those who had tried to leave Islam—eighty thousand people. This is how Abu Bakr followed the example of Muhammad.

The example of Jesus and His friends

At the end of His life, Jesus was arrested in front of His disciples by a mob armed with swords and clubs. One of His disciples pulled out a sword to defend Him, but Jesus told him, "Put your sword back in its place . . . for all who draw the sword will die by the sword" (Matt. 26:52).

The mob arrested Jesus, and He was killed. He was in the grave for three days. Then He rose from the dead and appeared to the disciples. His final instructions were:

Go into all the world and preach the good news to all creation. Whoever believes and is baptized will be saved, but whoever does not believe will be condemned. And these signs will accompany those who believe: In my name they will drive out demons; they will speak in new tongues; they will pick up snakes with their hands; and when they drink deadly poison, it will not hurt them at all; they will place their hands on sick people, and they will get well.

—MARK 16:15–17

The disciples went back to Jerusalem. After they received the Holy Spirit on the Day of Pentecost, they began to preach with boldness. They performed healings and other miracles.

At the same time, they were persecuted by many groups of people—Jews, Romans and idol worshipers—put in prison, threatened and beaten. All but one of the twelve disciples were killed because of their faith.

Not one time did Jesus' followers try to organize political or military protection for themselves. This is how the disciples followed the example of Jesus.

What about the Old Testament?

If you know the Old Testament, you may be thinking, *In the Old Testament, many times God commanded the children of Israel to fight. For example, see Deuteronomy 20:10–15.*

I must answer this question from the Christian point of view. In the time of the Old Testament, God gave mankind the Law. The Law said that if you sinned, you must be punished. It was eye for eye, tooth for tooth (Exod. 21:24).

God used people and nations to fulfill this principle. Therefore, when the nations living around Israel were full of sin, God commanded the Israelites to punish them (by military attack, for example). When the children of Israel were in sin, God used their neighbors to punish them as well.

Jesus expressed the principle of the Law this way: He who lives by the sword will die by the sword. (See Matthew 26:52.) In other words, if you attack other people, they will attack you. This was justice under Old Testament Law.

The Crusades were an example of this principle in action. The Crusaders punished the Muslims with the same sword the Muslims had used against others. This does not justify what the Roman Catholic Church did, but we can see what purpose it served.

The Catholic Church also felt the sharp side of the two-edged sword. God took away its power through the Reformation and Martin Luther.

Through Jesus, God gave people a new way of justice. Jesus taught:

> You have heard that it was said, "Eye for eye, and tooth for tooth." But I tell you, Do not resist an evil person. If someone strikes you on the right cheek, turn to him the other also. And if someone wants to sue you and take your tunic, let him have your cloak as well. If someone forces you to go one mile, go with him two miles. Give to the one who asks you, and do not turn away from the one who wants to borrow from you.
> —MATTHEW 5:38–42

In conclusion, a Christian cannot use the Old Testament to justify a holy war (like the Crusades) because Jesus took away the law of eye for eye, tooth for tooth. He replaced it with humility, laying down your rights and your power. Jesus practiced this in His own life. The Bible records:

> He humbled himself and became obedient to death— even death on a cross! Therefore God exalted him to the highest place.
> —PHILIPPIANS 2:8–9

CONCLUSION

Christians cannot justify fighting and killing in the name of God by their Bible or by the example of Jesus. Any time Christians do these sorts of things, they are going against their faith. On the other hand, Muslims *can* justify fighting and killing in the name of Allah by the Quran and by the example of Muhammad. When Muslims do these sorts of things, they are being good followers of their faith.

Section summary

You've just covered fourteen hundred years of history between the Muslims and the Jews. We are now going to look at the events that started a new phase in the unfinished battle—the Jews returning to present-day Israel and establishing their own country.

SECTION 6

PHASE FOUR OF THE UNFINISHED BATTLE: THE BATTLE ESCALATES AS JEWS ESTABLISH THE STATE OF ISRAEL (1898 TO PRESENT)

CHAPTER 20

A Call to War for Islam

YOU DON'T HAVE TO DECLARE WAR when you are already the winner.

That was the situation between Muslims and Jews until the very end of the nineteenth century. Jews were scattered all over the world. They were no threat to Islam. But something changed.

The Jews returned to present-day Israel.

And Islam declared that the unfinished battle must be fought with new vigor.

In this chapter, you will see how the declaration of the state of Israel set off the chain of events that has led to the modern terrorism we see today. Here is a brief overview of what happened.

* Jews began to return to present-day Israel in 1917, and Israel declared statehood in 1948.

* Various Muslim nations joined together to attack Israel and were defeated several times— in 1948, 1956, 1967 and 1973.

* Their losses were blamed on the leadership's lack of submission to Islam.

* Even though the president of Egypt made peace with Israel in 1978, Muslim nations and people refused to accept it.

* Terrorist groups went back to the Quran and

committed themselves to fighting the unfinished battle against Israel.

Now let's look at these events in detail and see how the
fight against Israel was continuously pushed forward by the
teachings of Islam.

JEWS RETURN TO THEIR HOMELAND

In 1897, Theodor Herzl organized the First Zionist
Congress in Basel, Switzerland, to discuss how Jewish
people could return to Israel and establish their own state. At
that time the land of present-day Israel was part of the
Islamic state, so Herzl went to the Muslim caliph (leader) in
Turkey and made a proposal. Herzl offered to give the
Islamic state some money to help with their financial trou-
bles in return for the caliph allowing the Jewish people to
immigrate to present-day Israel as a first step to establishing
their own state there. The Muslim caliph refused, and
Theodore Herzl started to look for another way.[1]

About fifteen years later, Turkey aligned itself with the
Central Powers during World War I, and their side was
defeated. Great Britain took control of the land that is now
present-day Israel. When this happened, the Jewish leaders
went to the British government and received permission
from them to settle in the land and to establish a political
state. (This is known as the Balfour Declaration of 1917.)

Jews from all over the world began to go to Israel. They
started practicing normal life there, opening businesses,
building farms, creating organizations. They established a
protective police force to defend themselves against people
around them.

While Israeli infrastructure was developing, the organization of the Muslim world was eroding. In 1924, the

government in Turkey was overthrown. A secular government was established under Kamil Attaturk. The former Turkish government had served as both the government of Turkey and as the ruling authority for the Muslim world. It had united Muslim countries under a centralized government. Now the central government was gone, and Muslim countries were under the domination of Western colonial powers such as Great Britain, France and Italy.

Because of the problems in their own countries, Muslims didn't react to what the Jews were doing in present-day Israel. That would change in 1948.

ISRAEL OFFICIALLY DECLARES STATEHOOD

In 1948, Ben-Gurion, one of the Jewish leaders, made an official declaration that the state of Israel was established. In response, the Islamic/Arabic world erupted like a volcano.[2] The call of jihad was pronounced throughout the Islamic/Arab world. The first call to jihad came from founder of the Muslim Brotherhood in Egypt (the forerunner of the today's terrorist organizations). Al-Azhar also openly condemned Israel. All the people in the Arab countries were pushing their governments to send their militaries to fight Israel.

Thousands volunteered for service in the militaries of Syria, Egypt, Iraq, Lebanon and Jordan. In less than a year, these armies went to Israel to destroy this new state, but they were defeated. Israel had better equipment and weapons and prevailed in strategy. This was called the War of 1948.

DEALING WITH THEIR FIRST DEFEAT
AT THE HAND OF ISRAEL

When the defeated armies returned to their homes, there was great disappointment among Arab and Muslim people. The Muslim Brotherhood told the people:

Arabs/Muslims, you cannot win this battle between you and the Jews without Islam. Islam must rule your battle against Israel. Your military forces were defeated because they were secular. You were just fighting for the land. The real battle is not just a fight for land; it is a fight between Islam and Judaism.[3]

Let me explain three key points they were making. The Muslim Brotherhood said:

* The leadership and government of Muslim countries were secular because they were not based on Islamic principles alone. The governments had Western influences, such as European legal practices and non-Islamic ways of education. The print media were also not submitted to Islam. They were publishing articles about sex and Hollywood movies and printing pictures of women instead of focusing on Islamic issues. The Brotherhood believed these things damaged the new Muslim generation, taking them far from Islam.[4]

* Because of the secular leadership, the Muslim countries were losing their fight against Israel.

* It was not a fight for land. It was a fight to defend the religion of Islam against the religion of Judaism.

Under the leadership of Gamal Abdel Nasser, the fanatic Muslims overthrew the king of Egypt in 1952. Their goal was to use the Egyptian military to defeat the Jews under the banner of Islam.

The Muslim Brotherhood leaders wanted Nasser to declare an Islamic state in Egypt. When Nasser refused, they tried to assassinate him but failed. Nasser would spend much of his time as a leader in routing out and killing members of the Muslim Brotherhood, the same group that helped bring him to power.

THE WAR OVER THE CANAL

Nasser got involved in battle with Israel four years after he came to power, but he didn't attack Israel directly. The war was a result of a fight over control of the Suez Canal. The French had built the canal, which went through Egyptian land, and Egypt had signed an agreement that the French could control it for one hundred years. The channel provided the only shipping access between the Mediterranean Sea and the Indian Ocean. Despite the agreement, Nasser declared that Egypt would take control of the Suez Canal in 1956. In response, France and Great Britain joined together to attack Egypt, and Israel helped them.

The attack against Egypt was very successful. France was very close to gaining control of the canal again. However, the United States convinced them to back down. Egypt kept control of the canal and still has control of it today.

Nasser claimed that Egypt won a victory.

THE SIX-DAY WAR

After wiping out most of the Muslim Brotherhood in Egypt, Nasser focused on organizing the Islamic world for an attack against Israel.

Nasser had two famous slogans: "We will fight Israel and the one who stands behind Israel [referring to the United States]." "We will throw Israel into the sea." As a little child, I remember thousands of people gathering in the streets to hear Nasser's speeches.

Israel became aware of Nasser's plan and chose not to wait to be attacked. On June 5, 1967, the Israeli military surprised

Nasser and the other Arab leaders by simultaneously attacking Egypt, Syria and Jordan. It only took six days. The Israeli military absolutely destroyed the Egyptian, Syrian and Jordanian armed forces, taking the Golan Heights from Syria, the West Bank from Jordan and the Sinai Desert from Egypt.

After Israel's victory, large numbers of Palestinians left Israeli territory and went to countries throughout the Arabic world, including Jordan, Egypt, Iraq, Syria and Tunisia.

This Six-Day War forced Muslims in Egypt and all of the Middle East to go back to the Quran as the only source of understanding how the relationship between Muslims and Jews should be. Even the secular Muslims and governments in these countries welcomed this return to the Quran.

The Arabic media started to focus on Quranic teaching about Jews and Judaism They constantly presented the Quranic verses that say Jews are evil people who hate Islam.

WAR IN 1973

Nasser died, and Anwar al-Sadat was elected the new president of Egypt. Sadat rebuilt the Egyptian military and prepared for doing a final battle with the Jews. On October 6, 1973, the Egyptian and Syrian military initiated a surprise attack against the Israeli military. The world thought that this would be the end of Israel.

Sadat was close to winning the war, but after two weeks, Ariel Sharon, who was in charge of the Israeli army, executed an excellent bit of war strategy. He came between the Egyptian army and Cairo and cut off communication. The Israeli military defeated the Egyptian and Syrian militaries once again. In Egypt it is known as the *October War*. In the West it is known as the *Yom Kippur War*.

The United Nations and the United States helped Israel and Egypt to start peace negotiations. Ordinary Muslims felt confused and lost, but they knew one thing for sure: They would not accept peace with Israel. The Arab countries united together against Sadat and tried to stop him from making peace with Israel.

Saddam Hussein of Iraq called for the Conference of Resistance, inviting Arabic countries to discuss the issue in Baghdad, Iraq.[5] During this conference, the Arab leaders could not get Sadat to change his mind, so they cut their diplomatic ties with Egypt. Sadat walked the road of peace alone. He signed the Camp David agreement in 1978 and established normal relations between Israel and Egypt for the first time in modern history. For the promise of peace, Israel returned the Sinai Desert to Egypt.

REBELLION AGAINST SECULAR ISLAM

After the signing of the Camp David agreement, a great rebellion started in Egypt and the different countries of the Middle East. This Islamic rebellion came like waves and became stronger and stronger, especially after the Islamic revolution in Iran in 1979. Iran gave support to the Muslim radical groups, declaring that Israel and America were the greatest enemies of the Islamic world. Their goal was to throw out the secular governments of the Middle East and replace them with Islamic governments, as Iran had done.

Until then it had been secular militaries and governments that had attacked Israel. Now Islam rose up and turned the battle back to its religious roots. The jihad movement was born.

MORE JIHAD GROUPS FORM TO FIGHT ISRAEL

The Islamic movements like Muslim Brotherhood, Islamic Jihad, *al-Gama'a al-Islamiyya*, Hizbollah and Hamas gained momentum, convincing millions of people in the region that secular militaries would not be able to win the battle with the Jews. The jihad groups called Sadat an infidel, an apostate from Islam. They accused him of shaking hands with the pigs and the monkeys. They said, "We must let Islam rule our countries, taking authority and writing a new page in the history of the battle between the Muslims and the Jews."

Before the war in 1973, Sadat tried to use the media to prepare the Egyptian nation to fight Israel. Now he tried to use the media to turn the people toward peace. The media stopped using the aggressive Quranic verses toward Jews and replaced them with nice and peaceful Quranic verses from the first half of Muhammad's revelation. This strategy had no success. In many ways the Egyptian people clearly expressed that they would never normalize relations with Israel or put their hands in the hands of the Jewish people.

THE PEOPLE CONTINUE THE UNFINISHED BATTLE

After Camp David, some Israeli tourists came to Egypt with hope that a new relationship had been established between Israel and Egypt. They came full of desire to see the pyramids, the Nile River and the different places where their grandfathers lived centuries earlier. They came, but they were met with rejection. The bus carrying Israeli tourists in the city of Ismailia was attacked by Islamic fundamentalists, who shot and killed many Israelis.

In Tahrir Square in Cairo, an Egyptian fundamentalist group member saw a young Jewish man kiss his girlfriend in public, and he took his knife and killed the young man.

Also, I cannot forget the Egyptian soldier who was stationed on the border of Egypt and Israel in the Sinai Desert during the month of Ramadan (the month of fasting). One afternoon he saw a group of Jewish girls wearing just T-shirts and shorts. They weren't covered well by Islamic standards.

This soldier felt that the girls were attacking him with loose morality, so he took his gun and started shooting at them, killing all seven.

Only three years after the peace agreement was signed, Muslim militants successfully assassinated Sadat and attempted to take over Egypt (1981). They were stopped by the quick military action of Sadat's vice president, Hosni Mubarak, who is still president (in 2002).

CONCLUSION

Once again you can see how the teachings of Islam drive Muslims to fight Israel. When secular Muslim governments tried to live at peace with Israel, jihad groups rose up to continue the battle. They declared that there will be no agreement, no peace and no acknowledgment of Israel.

Israel has successfully defended herself thus far. Now let's look at the current strategy being used against Israel in the conflict with the Palestinians. Is there any hope for resolving it?

CHAPTER 21

The Front Lines:
Palestinians vs. Israel

TODAY THE FRONT LINE OF THE unfinished battle between Islam and the Jews is obvious—it is the Palestinian/ Israeli conflict.

The question I want to answer in this chapter is this: Are Palestinians willing to find a way to live in peace and harmony with Jews as their neighbors? Someone might say, "Only a Palestinian can answer this question."

First of all, remember that the majority of Palestinians are Arab *Muslims*, which means they are controlled by what the Quran and Islam teach them. This is where I came from, and this is what I learned and taught before I met the Lord Jesus Christ. I can answer these questions because I can explain the opinion of the Muslim scholars in the Middle East.

I am not going to look at this issue from the Jewish point of view or even from the Christian point of view. I am not going to refer to biblical teachings in this chapter. I am not going to go back in history and document all the people who have lived in the land of present-day Israel.

No, I am going to focus on the Muslim point of view, because when you see the Muslim point of view, you will understand the seriousness of the battle Israel faces.

First, in this chapter you will learn about two key beliefs that keep Muslims in never-ending conflict with the state of Israel. They are:

* A belief that the land belongs to Islam
* A belief that the holy mosque in Jerusalem must be kept pure

Then you will see the inevitable result of these beliefs:

* No peace negotiation is acceptable.
* Israel as a nation must be destroyed.

THE LAND BELONGS TO ISLAM

To understand the roots of this situation you have to look at it from a religious point of view. You cannot look at this situation and just say, "This is about Palestinians wanting a place to live." Of course, that is part of the issue, but that is not what makes the conflict so difficult to resolve.

From the Muslim point of view, the land of present-day Israel does not belong to any group of people—it belongs to Islam. Therefore, when the Jewish people declared the birth of the nation of Israel, it was an affront to every Islamic country because it took the land away from Islam.

The groups that are fighting against Israel and her allies express this point of view very clearly. Hamas, the largest, most active jihad group fighting in Israel, has a thirty-six-article covenant that outlines its position toward Israel. Here are some excerpts:[1]

> The land of Palestine is an Islamic Waqf [Holy Possession] consecrated for future Moslem generations until Judgment Day. No one can renounce it or any part, or abandon it or any part of it.
>
> —ARTICLE 11

> Palestine is an Islamic land... Since this is the case, the Liberation of Palestine is an individual duty for every Moslem wherever he may be.
>
> —ARTICLE 13

In 2000, the Islamic Assembly of North America published a booklet titled *No for Normalization*, written by a Muslim scholar. He gave a similar picture of the Muslim view of land rights.

> The Jews came and attacked this land and stole it, and this will not change the fact that this land is Muslim, and it will remain that way forever. If we aren't able to liberate this land today from the Jews, this doesn't mean that we can give it up. We have to work until the time comes, and then we will bring it back to the Islamic world.[2]

THE HOLY SITE MUST BE KEPT PURE

Present-day Israel does not merely occupy Islamic territory. It also contains the third most holy site of Islam—the al-Aqsa Mosque in Jerusalem. This mosque was built by the second caliph of Islam, Umar ibn al-Khattab, and it has been in continuous use ever since.

Many Westerners do not understand how serious Muslims are about keeping their holy sites pure. A holy site must not be corrupted by the presence of non-Muslims, who are considered impure and unholy.

For example, until very recently, a non-Muslim was not allowed to go inside any mosque because of being impure. But that practice has recently changed to allow non-Muslims inside mosques so that Muslims can try to win them to Islam.

In Islam, a holy site must be defended. You didn't see Christians draw arms when Palestinian militants barricaded themselves in the Church of the Nativity in 2002, but if that had been a Muslim holy site, arms would have been drawn all over the Middle East.

Currently, Israel controls Jerusalem, but the Muslims are in control of the Al-Aqsa Mosque and the large compound that is built around it. This compound includes the Dome of the Rock mosque.* This location is also referred to as the Temple Mount because it is believed to be the site of Solomon's great temple. Herod, during the time of Jesus, also built a temple there.[3] The Muslims have built a wall all around the compound, and non-Muslims are not permitted inside that wall.

The fact that infidels (non-Muslims) are living and working all around the al-Aqsa Mosque infuriates committed Muslims, including Osama bin Laden. He declared in his 1998 *fatwa* against America and Israel:

> The ruling to kill the Americans and their allies— civilians and military—is an individual duty for every Muslim who can do it in any country in which it is possible to do it, *in order to liberate the al-Aqsa Mosque and the holy mosque [the Kaaba in Mecca] from their grip, and in order for their armies to move out of all the lands of Islam,* defeated and unable to threaten any Muslim.[4]
>
> —EMPHASIS ADDED

The liberation of holy sites is not just an excuse that Islamic groups use to cover up their real motive. It *is* their real motive.

From the Muslim point of view, it is not enough that Muslims are actually in control of the mosque sites. The impure, corrupting presence of non-Muslim Americans and Jews must also be cleansed from the area.

WHAT MAKES THE AL-AQSA MOSQUE HOLY?

Would you like to know what makes the al-Aqsa Mosque so holy? It is because of an event known in Islam as the *Night*

---

* Sometimes the entire compound is referred to as the Dome of the Rock.

Journey. Here is how it is recorded in Islamic history.

Muhammad woke up one morning and told his followers that Allah had taken him on an amazing journey. He said that during the night, the angel Gabriel had come to him with a mule. Muhammad rode this mule through the air from Mecca, where he was living, to Jerusalem. In Jerusalem he found the prophets of Allah waiting for him on the ground at the site where the Jewish temple had stood. Muhammad led all the prophets in Islamic prayers.

Then the angel Gabriel took Muhammad on another journey to heaven to meet with Allah. In his meetings with Allah, Muhammad negotiated the mandatory number of prayers down from fifty times a day to five times a day. The angel Gabriel also took Muhammad to visit hell. Muhammad told his people that hell was mostly populated with women. He saw one woman who was in hell because she locked her cat in a room without food and water. Another woman was hanging by chains from the ceiling because she committed adultery.

Before the end of the night, Muhammad flew on the mule back to Mecca.

The details of the story you just read are recorded in hadith, but Muhammad received a Quranic revelation about it as well.

> Glorified (and Exalted) be He (Allah) [above all that (evil) they associate with Him] Who took His slave (Muhammad) for a journey by night from *Al-Masjid-al-Haram* (at Makkah) to *Al-Masjid-al-Aqsa* (in Jerusalem), the neighborhood whereof We have blessed, in order that We might show him (Muhammad) of Our *Ayat* (proofs, evidences, lessons, signs, etc.).
>
> —SURAH 17:1

When the Islamic military conquered Jerusalem less than two years after the death of Muhammad, they remembered the story of the night journey. The leader ordered his military to find the site of the old temple and to build a mosque on it. They called it the *al-Aqsa Mosque,* meaning, "the far mosque."

THE JEWS AND THE MOSQUE

Some groups of Jews want to rebuild the temple on the site where the ancient temple stood. To do this, they must destroy the mosque on the site. Many different attempts have been made, especially by Orthodox Jews. The mosque has been "invaded" many times by Jews who go inside to lead prayers. Numerous bombing attempts have been uncovered, and gunmen have shot at the Dome of the Rock several times.

My point is that Jewish people will keep trying to get control of the Dome of the Rock until they are successful. It is just a matter of time, in my opinion.[5]

When Jews succeed in taking over the Dome of the Rock, the reaction in the Muslim world is going to be disaster. We can make this prediction by looking at the great conflict over a mosque in India that isn't even a special holy site.

When the Islamic army invaded India in the seventh century, they built a mosque on top of the site of a holy Hindu temple, considered to be the birthplace of one of the Hindu gods. Hindus destroyed the mosque in 1992, and Muslims killed thousands of Hindus in retaliation. Nevertheless, Hindus kept control of the site and began to build a temple. In 2002, a mob of Muslims stoned and fired upon a train of Hindu pilgrims who had just visited the site. As a result, fifty-eight people died, and several hundred were wounded. This event sparked fights between Muslims and Hindu activists all over India.[6]

You can see that Muslims vigorously defend every mosque. If the third most holy mosque in the world were taken away from them, the whole Islamic world would be ignited. The first clash would be between the Muslims and the governments. The people would insist that the governments act, while the secular governments would want to wait and negotiate. Terrorist groups would step up attacks on Israel and her allies in retaliation. Many people have the potential to be drawn into this conflict.

NEGOTIATION IS NOT ACCEPTABLE

Western powers are trying to get Palestinians and Jews to sit down at the negotiating table all the time. However, from the Muslim point of view, no negotiation is acceptable.

> Palestine is a part of the land of the Muslim world; no one has any right to give it to any other group of people than those to whom it rightfully belongs, i.e. the entire Muslim world.
>
> A Muslim has the right to give up his own land or property by giving it away to others, or selling it, but here Muslims have no right to give away this Muslim land in Palestine to the Jews because it doesn't belong to them; it belongs to Islam.[7]

The world sees what happens when peace talks are led by the United Nations and the United States. Whenever Arafat or his representatives meet with Israel, Islamic fundamentalist groups bomb and kill Israelis. They say that Arafat does not represent the Muslims and Arabs in this struggle. They see him as just a political man looking for a little piece of land to establish a little state called the state of Palestine. It doesn't matter if it's in the Gaza Strip or the West Bank.

When Arafat signed an agreement with Israel at the Madrid Conference in 1991, the Islamic groups were very upset. They proclaimed that Arafat had no right to sign an agreement giving up land.

The Muslim fundamentalist groups in the Middle East understand and practice true Islam and have the full Islamic picture of the relationship between Muslims and Jews. They will never be satisfied by what Arafat is looking for. Their point of view about peace agreements can be summed up this way:

> We do not accept these agreements with the Jews because if we accept them, it will take us away from the practice of jihad, which is the highest calling of our faith. We cannot stop practicing our animosity toward the Jews because we are commanded by the Quranic verses to continue hating the Jews and believing that they are the worst enemies of ours until the end of time.[8]

Negotiation will not work because that is the political solution. Political solutions work for political problems. For example, the problem of apartheid in South Africa was solved by a political solution because it was a political problem. There was no religious foundation to it. But the problem between Islam and Israel is a religious problem from the Muslim point of view.

ELIMINATION OF ISRAEL

The only acceptable solution, from the Muslim point of view, is to eliminate Israel. As the Covenant of the Hamas states:

> The Islamic Resistance Movement is a distinguished Palestinian movement, whose allegiance is to Allah, and whose way of life is Islam. It strives to raise the banner of Allah over every inch of Palestine.
> —ARTICLE 6[9]

> Israel will exist and will continue to exist until Islam will obliterate it, just as it obliterated others before it.
> —PREAMBLE TO THE COVENANT OF HAMAS[10]

It is not just the radical jihad groups who make these kinds of statements. They are preached in mosques throughout the Islamic world. You can go to a website on the Internet that gives you the English translation of some of these sermons (www.alminbar.net). In a recent message at a major mosque in al-Riyadh in the Kingdom of Saudi Arabia, the sheikh stated:

> Today the Islamic nation already knows that the Holy Land will not be liberated by dallying at vacation sites or sitting around the negotiating table with infidels. The solution is to do what the Prophet did to the Jews when they violated the agreements. The solution regarding the Jews is as the Prophet Muhammad said: "I have brought slaughter upon you." Yes, the solution for these is not peace and harmony. Jihad, not peace, is the solution.[11]

A book published in the United States declared:

> Every Muslim must believe that it's a very high calling from Allah in his life to go and to fight and to kill the Jews.[12]

The Christian Broadcasting Network recorded an interview with a Muslim sheikh in England. In that interview they asked him what he thought about Israel. He responded with a metaphor that jihad groups have been using for decades: Israel is a cancer planted by the Western countries and the United States. It's the responsibility of Muslims everywhere to participate in the effort to remove Israel completely.[13]

MUSLIM UNDERSTANDING OF SUICIDE MISSIONS

The Palestinian fight against Israel is supported by the highest levels of Islamic religious authority. The Great Imam of Al-Azhar (comparable in status to the pope of the Roman Catholic Church) was interviewed after the first female

Palestinian suicide bomber blew herself up. He made this statement: "Every Palestinian person—man or woman—who blows himself up will be a martyr."[14]

Martyrdom is a technical religious term. A martyr will go directly to Paradise—no waiting in the grave like other Muslims; no judging on Judgment Day; Paradise guaranteed.

Islam teaches Muslims that if they fight jihad they cannot lose. If they get killed, they are martyrs and go to Paradise. If they win, they enjoy the victory. There is no way to lose a battle fought for Islam.

The West calls them suicide bombings. But to Muslims, this is not suicide. This is fighting. Jihad is to kill or die—not just to kill, but also to die.

Killing for jihad is totally different from committing a murder. Islam makes a clear distinction between the two. Islam condemns lawless killing in society. But it upholds killing in jihad. (See chapter nine.)

CONCLUSION

Now you can see what Palestinian Muslims believe about their fight against Israel. Is it any wonder that peace has not been found! In the next short chapter, I want to give you a very unique perspective on this situation. You know a lot about the way Muslims feel toward Israel. There is another side to the Muslim psyche. You need to understand how Muslims believe that the Jews feel toward them.

CHAPTER 22

Muslims Believe
Jews Hate Them

MUSLIMS HAVE A WELL-DEVELOPED ATTITUDE and rationale about the Jewish people. They are taught in the Quran, in hadith, by tradition, by culture, in school, at home, in the café and on the street. They know for sure that Jews are their number one enemy. Muslims also believe that Jews have the same feelings against them. To put it bluntly, Muslims believe the Jews hate Islam and want to destroy it.

Dr. Mustafa Mahmoud, one of the most popular writers in the Arabic world today, wrote that Jews want to "pull up Islam by its roots." He claimed that the Jewish involvement in the Battle of the Trench was their first attempt to eradicate Islam. He also wrote that the Jews are behind wars all over the world with the motive of destroying Islam. Other Muslim writers share his views.[1]

Muslims believe that Jews have a long list of reasons for wanting to destroy Islam. An Islamic professor listed those reasons in his book, *Threatening and Challenging*. They include:

*   The Jews are mad because God rejected them as His chosen people and chose the Muslims instead.

*   The Quran has exposed to the world that Jews are the source of all evil.

* Muhammad was more powerful than all the Jewish prophets before him. He was the final prophet, and the Quran was the final revelation.

* Muhammad destroyed the Jewish settlements and forced them to leave Arabia.

* The Muslim scholars proved they are more powerful and honest and faithful than the Jewish rabbis because Muslim scholars never tried to change the Holy Quran. They claimed Jewish rabbis changed the Word of God and replaced it with their own words, thus forfeiting the position and the authority that was given them by God.

* During their history of battles and wars, Muslim soldiers and fighters proved to be stronger than Jewish soldiers (until modern times when secular Muslims were fighting Israel).

* Jews know that a strong Jewish state and a strong Islamic state cannot exist together at the same time.

* Muslims would not allow the Jews to establish a new state on their lands, and they would not let the Jews have the Temple Mount.

According to this Muslim author, the above reasons come together to make Jewish hatred toward Muslims complete. In other words, he thinks that Jews consider Muslims to be their worst enemy.[2]

I am sad to say that all these things were what I believed when I was practicing Islam in Egypt. I was a product of Islam, and my heart had been poisoned. I believed the Jews were engaged in an unfinished battle against Islam.

Let me conclude by saying that I have learned that most

Jews do *not* have hatred against Muslims. Most Jews just want to be allowed to live their lives and practice their faith. They don't mind Muslims practicing their faith as long as Muslims do not cause harm to the Jewish people.

The Jewish Scriptures do not teach hatred toward Islam. They don't even mention Islam, because Islam didn't exist at the time they were written.

A lot of Jews in Israel are very frustrated by the Palestinians, but they are not trying to destroy the religion of Islam.

THE PICTURE IS COMPLETE

Now I believe you have a good understanding of the foundation underneath the relationship between Islam and the Jews today. The next section of the book will be very exciting, because it tells how these two groups can be brought together.

Section 7

How Muslims and Jews
Can Be Reconciled

CHAPTER 23

The Way to Peace

WHO IS GOING TO STOP THE violence, the suicide and the bloodshed in the Middle East? I can say for sure that it is not the United Nations, it is not the United States of America, and it is not more peace talks. There is no power in this world that is able to clean the hearts of Muslims and bring reconciliation between them and the Jews except the blood of Jesus Christ.

When I look back to those years that I lived, studied and taught Islam, I see the darkness in which I was living. I was indoctrinated by the Quran, and I had no idea that the only source of peace for this world is the Prince of Peace, the Lord Jesus Christ.

When I was a Muslim, Jesus was just a prophet to me, just a man, like many men who were chosen by God to deliver His message to the world, but they couldn't change the world. They couldn't reconcile people with each other. They couldn't take hatred away from the hearts of evil people. They couldn't change lives. They couldn't bring the dead back to life. Only God can do this.

But I praise the Lord that after meeting Him I received the truth, and I started to see the true nature of Jesus, that He is the living God and the Prince of Peace. Then I knew that peace was possible in the world through Jesus Christ.

JESUS *IS* PEACE

I remember how amazed and excited I was when I read Ephesians 2:11–21 for the first time. It was during the time when I was receiving victory over the old Muslim man inside me at Youth With A Mission in South Africa. I saw the reality of my life in the words of these verses.

Paul was writing to Gentiles in Ephesus. He wanted them to understand that their relationship with Christ also changed their relationship with the people around them, particularly the Jews. First Paul reminded them:

> Therefore, remember that formerly you who are Gentiles by birth and called "uncircumcised" by those who call themselves "the circumcision"…remember that at that time you were separate from Christ, excluded from citizenship in Israel and foreigners to the covenants of promise, without hope and without God in the world. But now in Christ Jesus you who were once far away have been brought near through the blood of Christ.
>
> —EPHESIANS 2:11–13

As a Muslim, I was just like Paul's description of the Gentiles. I was "far away" from God, without hope. But God brought me near to Himself, and in doing that, He brought me near to His people, the Jews. I love what Paul wrote next. It's about how Jesus makes peace between two former enemies—the Gentiles and the Jews.

> For he himself is our peace, who has made the two one and has destroyed the barrier, the dividing wall of hostility, by abolishing in his flesh the law with its commandments and regulations. His purpose was to create in himself one new man out of the two, thus making peace, and in this one body to reconcile both of them to God through the cross, by which he put to death

their hostility. He came and preached peace to you who were far away and peace to those who are near.
—Ephesians 2:14–17

Do you see this most wonderful picture of reconciliation? Jesus' blood shed on the cross two thousand years ago was for reconciliation. Jesus made peace not only between man and God, but also between man and man.

Jesus preached peace to those far away (Gentiles) and to those who were near (Jews). Through Himself, He made one out of two; he made the two groups, Jews and Gentiles, into one people. He destroyed "the dividing wall of hostility" between these peoples. He "put hostility to death."

By my life experience, I can witness this is the Word of God. God practiced this Word in my life. I know where I came from as a Muslim, and I know the love in my heart toward Jewish people now. Just as Jesus brings together Gentiles and Jews, He brings together Muslims and Jews.

There is a totally new picture when people come together through Jesus Christ. Paul explained:

> Consequently, you are no longer foreigners and aliens, but fellow citizens with God's people and members of God's household, built on the foundation of the apostles and prophets, with Christ Jesus himself as the chief cornerstone. In him the whole building is joined together and rises to become a holy temple in the Lord.
> —Ephesians 2:19–21

When I became a Christian, I became part of one household that included Jews and every other person who believes Jesus is the Son of God. All together we are a holy temple unto the Lord. This is the picture of peace.

Finally, let's see who lives in this holy temple, built out of people who were former enemies.

167

> You . . . are being built together to become a dwelling in which God lives by his Spirit.
>
> —EPHESIANS 2:22

Jews, Gentiles, former Muslims, atheists, idol worshipers—as followers of Jesus we become one temple where the Spirit of God lives.

CHAPTER 24

The Calling of the Church

IT IS SO WONDERFUL TO HAVE hope for the situation between Muslims and Jews because Jesus is the way to peace.

At the same time, this is a great challenge to those of us who are Christians. We can't just sit back and allow Jews and Muslims to continue as they are.

Here is how the church can reach them.

1. *Accept the Great Commission that Jesus gave:* "Go and make disciples of all nations" (Matt. 28:19). This includes reaching out to both Muslims and Jews.

2. *Prepare.* The church needs to raise up workers who are called for this specific mission. They will need special training and equipping before they go to the field. The church will have to set aside some of its budget to fund these missions and to provide for the needs of the workers.

3. *Support.* The missionaries on the front line must have prayer warriors to support them. Some of these prayer warriors need to move from the home church to the front lines, spending time with the workers, praying with them, asking the Lord to give them strength and opportunity to share the Good News. The prayer warriors also need to pray in the field

itself, claiming the salvation of God to take place in this land amongst these people.

4. *Cooperate*. Whenever possible, the church should work in cooperation with former Muslims and Messianic Jews. They know their peoples, lands and cultures, and they know how to present the truth to them.

5. *Be wise*. Some Muslim governments have laws against trying to convert a Muslim. This cannot stop evangelism, but it will change its methods.

MOST EFFECTIVE METHODS

There are many different groups that are already spreading the Good News among Muslims, and I thank God for them. Each group has its favorite method, with varying degrees of effectiveness.

One time I was with a man in South Africa who worked in Muslim evangelism. I went with him to a hotel where we met some Muslims from that area. My friend handed the Muslim leader a copy of the New Testament. The Muslim leader left us and went to the kitchen. In my spirit, I knew exactly what was happening. He was throwing that Bible in the trash. I went after him into the kitchen and started looking for the trash can. When I found it, the Bible was inside.

"Why didn't you just tell my friend that you didn't want his Bible?" I asked him.

He had no answer for me, but I knew he would never tolerate someone doing something like that to him. I said, "What would happen if you gave me a copy of the Quran, and I threw it in the trash?"

He said, "I would kill you."

My point is that just handing a Muslim a Bible is not very

likely to win him over. This is because he already has too much resistance built up toward other beliefs. He is not going to open a Bible unless his heart has already been prepared to hear the gospel.

Why do Muslims have such strong defenses against the Good News? From their point of view, they don't need it. They already worship God. They have a holy book. They have a history. Islam is their life. It's is not just something they do in the mosque. Their culture and their religion are completely mixed together.

This is solid rock. How are we going to move this rock?

I believe the best method for Muslim evangelism is building relationships one-on-one. I would advise you not to speak to even a small group of Muslims, because none of them will want to appear to question Islam in front of the others. This setting just opens the door for a big argument because the Quran teaches Muslims to argue.

So again, I believe the best way to reach a Muslim is one-on-one. Give some thought to those with whom you speak. Friendships should be man to man, woman to woman, young to young and old to old.

It will be hard work, and you will have to answer many questions. As I said earlier, people who are working on the front lines with Muslims need prayer support. One of the biggest challenges you will face is the spirit of religion. Let's look at what the Bible says about the spirit of religion.

THE SPIRIT OF RELIGION

No matter where you find Muslims (in the West or the East), you will see the spirit of religion in operation. Intercessors need to ask God to control this spirit so that the Good News can reach the hearts of the people.

The spirit of religion is the way Satan deceives people into

171

thinking that they are pleasing God when they are actually just doing what seems good to them. It's about doing religious things instead of doing what God wants.

Muslims spend much time and energy practicing their religion, but they are never pleasing God. This is Satan's great deception in their lives.

THE SPIRIT OF RELIGION AMONG BELIEVERS

You will even find the spirit of religion among people who are worshiping the God of the Bible. The most powerful chapter in the Bible exposing the spirit of religion is Isaiah 58. God's people were doing fasts, thinking that God would be pleased, but God was not responding to them (v. 3). Why? God explained:

> Yet on the day of your fasting, you do as you please
>   and exploit all your workers.
> Your fasting ends in quarreling and strife,
>   and in striking each other with wicked fists.
> You cannot fast as you do today
>   and expect your voice to be heard on high.
> —ISAIAH 58:3–4

In other words, your acts of service to God are not acceptable when you are fighting with the people around you. God wants more than people performing religious duties. He said:

> Is not this the kind of fasting I have chosen:
> to loose the chains of injustice
>   and untie the cords of the yoke,
> to set the oppressed free
>   and break every yoke?
> Is it not to share your food with the hungry
>   and to provide the poor wanderer with
>   shelter—
> when you see the naked, to clothe him,

and not to turn away from your own flesh
and blood?…
Then you will call, and the Lord will answer.
—ISAIAH 58:6–9

God told His people to look around them for those who are oppressed, those who are hungry, those without shelter or clothing. "Take care of these people, and you will please Me," He said.

Jesus ran into the spirit of religion in the Jewish temple. He was teaching there on the Sabbath day when He saw a woman who had been crippled by an evil spirit for eighteen years. Jesus healed her, and the religious Jewish leaders got very upset. They told the people, "There are six days for work. So come and be healed on those days, not on the Sabbath" (Luke 13:14).

They forgot they were not just talking to a man or a prophet. Jesus was God Himself, standing in front of them. He was the God of the Law of Moses.

Jesus said, "You hypocrites! Doesn't each of you on the Sabbath untie his ox or donkey from the stall and lead it out to give it water? Then should not this woman, a daughter of Abraham, whom Satan has kept bound for eighteen long years, be set free on the Sabbath day from what bound her?" (v. 15).

In this story Jesus fulfilled the Word of God in Isaiah 58. He showed again that God wants righteous people led by the Spirit of God, not people who are worshiping the law and forgetting the heart of mercy of God.

The spirit of religion is powerful among Muslims and Jews. It is found in many churches as well, including the church of the Middle East. In the next chapter I want to introduce you to the Middle Eastern church. It has had many struggles, but it is also in the best position to reach many Jews and Muslims who need the Good News.

CHAPTER 25

The Struggles of the Middle Eastern Church

ONE DAY I WAS ABOUT TO speak at an Arabic church in the United States, and the pastor mentioned in his introduction that I had been interviewed on *The 700 Club*. *The 700 Club* is the television ministry of Pat Robertson, who strongly supports Israel.

I got up to speak and was near the end of my message when an Arab man stood up and started accusing me. "Why did you accept the invitation to appear on *The 700 Club*? Don't you know who Pat Robertson is? This man is not a Christian. This man is a Zionist. This man is supporting Jews in Israel who kill our people and destroy our homes."

I was sure this man was a Muslim. I spoke to him kindly and said, "I am almost finished. After this meeting, let's go outside and have some coffee and talk about this." Later I spoke with the man and discovered to my shock that he was a Christian. I couldn't believe how much he sounded like a Muslim when he spoke about Israel.

Unfortunately, his attitude against Jews is very common in the church of the Middle East.

In this chapter, I pray for God to help me present to you the situation of the church in the Middle East. Western Christians may be surprised at how different this church is compared to the Western church.

THE MISSING EVANGELISTS

I believe the saddest thing about the church in the Middle East is that they are the missing evangelists. The church of the Middle East has the best opportunity to help reconcile Muslims and Jews by presenting them with the gospel. Unfortunately, this hasn't been happening.

The church of the Middle East doesn't want to reach out to Muslims or Jews. They avoid the Muslims because Christians are often persecuted for converting a Muslim. They avoid the Jews because they consider Jews to be their enemies—just as the Muslims do.

This attitude may surprise you. However, it helps to remember that the church of the Middle East has survived in the land of fire and focuses most of its energy toward not getting burned. It is in survival mode.

The Christians have been at the mercy of politics in the Middle East ever since Muhammad's army conquered their countries. Christian leaders are not free. They are under the shadow of the government. As a result, they have isolated themselves from the community. They don't want to take the risk of bringing anyone new into the church.

When I became a Christian in Egypt, I had a very hard time finding a church that would allow me to attend services. I went personally to three different pastors who told me that I was not welcome in their churches. I finally went to a monastery, far outside Cairo, hoping they would help me because they were far away from the secret police in the city. Even they refused, but they gave me the name of one more pastor who might help. I went to that church the next day. The pastor was very tough at first, trying to make sure I was honest. He did accept me, and I worshiped with that church for a year until I left Egypt.

I thank God for this pastor who was willing to take a big risk to reach out to a Muslim convert. I was careful not to cause him trouble. I took a bus to church instead of driving my car to avoid being followed by radical Muslims. I did not tell my story to members of the church. I also was careful not to get stopped by the Egyptian policeman who was assigned as a security guard at the door of the church. Until the policeman got used to seeing me, I was always careful to go in and out of the door mixed in with a large group of people.

As you can see just by my stories, the church exists under a lot of fear and intimidation. I believe this is part of the reason they have adopted the Muslim attitudes against Israel. It helps their relationship with Muslims a little bit. Here is a sample of what they believe.

OPPOSITION TO THE JEWS

Pope Shenuda, the leader of the Coptic Orthodox Church in Egypt, has done a good job of expressing the beliefs of the church about the Jews. Most Middle Eastern Christians share his beliefs (both orthodox and evangelical). In a series of interviews that were published in a book, he expressed the following ideas:

God is finished with the Jews.

Pope Shenuda said, "Our Christian religion says God is finished already with the Jews. As the chosen people, the Jews received the message of God and protected His books. The Christians have come and taken over that position . . . There is no place for the Jews in God's plan any more."[1]

The Jews do not have a divine right to present-day Israel.

Pope Shenuda was asked about the biblical references that speak of Jews returning to the Promised Land. He replied,

"The promise of God for Israel that is in the Bible speaks about the past, not the present. It wasn't a promise that dealt with their future. The promise was given to the Jews in the Old Testament, but not to the Jews in our present time."[2]

Muslims have more in common with Christians than the Jews because Muslims accept Jesus as a prophet and Jews do not.

Pope Shenuda said, "Islam believes that Jesus Christ came and was born of the Virgin Mary, and Islam believes the miracles done by Jesus, and the Quran describes this. Islam calls the Christians the People of the Book. Islam acknowledges us and respects us, but the Jews are denying every religion."[3]

Another Arabic leader in the Middle Eastern church made a similar statement. He asserted that God would be more supportive of Muslims than Jews for the following reason:

> The Jews have rejected Jesus and deny Him, but the Arab Muslims have never rejected Christ. They believe in Jesus. Why would God would take the side of the people who denied, rejected, and killed Jesus (i.e., the Jews), and turn against the people who believe in him as a prophet (i.e., the Muslims)?[4]

Christians should not visit Israel until Jerusalem is under the control of Arabs.

Pope Shenuda has forbidden Coptic Christians (the Orthodox Church of Egypt) to visit Israel. He reasoned:

1. If we visit Israel, it will say that we agree with what Israel is doing to the Arabs and Palestinians.
2. The money we spend in Israel will be a source of income for the Jews to use against the Arabs.

He declared, "I will not visit Jerusalem until it is delivered from the hands of the Jews into the hands of the Arabs. Then

I will go to Jerusalem with my hand in the hand of Sheikh Al-Azhar (the highest Muslim religious leader at Al-Azhar)."[5]

THE STRONGHOLD OF TRADITION/ SPIRIT OF RELIGION

Rejection of Old Testament

Because of their attitude toward the Jews, many Christians in the Middle East believe the Old Testament is no longer valid. A friend who pastors an Arabic church told me, "When I preached from the Old Testament, they would say, 'We don't believe it, and if you won't stop preaching from the Old Testament, we won't come back to your church ever again.'"

These Christians said the Old Testament was for the Jews only. They did not recognize that God used the Old Testament to speak to the whole world.

Influence of Arab culture on the Arabic Bible

Another big issue for the Middle Eastern church is what word is used for God in the Arabic language Christian Bible. Most Westerners will be shocked to learn what word is used for God the Father in the Arabic Bible. It is *Allah*. So John 3:16 reads, "For Allah so loved the world..." When the Arabic Bible refers to other parts of the Trinity, it says *Allah the Son* or *Allah the Holy Spirit*.

For myself, I hate this feature of the Arabic Bible. I was delivered from Islam, and I have no desire to read the name of Allah in my Bible. Hatred, destruction, killing, anger, deceit, racism and hopelessness—this is the name *Allah* to me.

However, Arab Christians say that they want to have the name *Allah* because it comes from their Arabic heritage. They say that the name *Allah* was being used in Arabia before Islam. However, the fact is that the name *Allah* has never referred to the one true God of heaven.

I share this issue with you to help you understand that there is a spirit of religion in the Middle Eastern church that needs to be changed. This is just one of its evidences.

Spirit of fear

Another great challenge for the church is the spirit of fear. I know a wonderful Christian Arab lady who is active in evangelism. She told me this story:

> My son came one day and asked me, "Mom, if a Muslim fanatic came to you and told you to convert to Islam, and that if you refused he will kill your children, what would you do?"
>
> I waited a minute, but I told him, "I will not deny Christ, even if he's going to threaten me to kill my children."
>
> My son left the room saying, "Mom, I am so happy to hear that from you and to know that me and my brothers cannot take the place of Jesus Christ in your life. Thank you, Mom. You gave me another lesson about what faith in Jesus Christ is like."

This family is literally living out this verse:

> Anyone who loves his father or mother more than me is not worthy of me; anyone who loves his son or daughter more than me is not worthy of me.
>
> —Matthew 10:37

The disciples were able to spread the Good News to the entire world because the blood of Jesus defeated Satan and destroyed the stronghold of the spirit of fear. Jesus told His disciples:

> Do not be afraid of those who kill the body but cannot kill the soul.
>
> —Matthew 10:28

Paul, who suffered great persecution, wrote:

> What is more, I consider everything a loss compared to
> the surpassing greatness of knowing Christ Jesus my
> Lord, for whose sake I have lost all things. I consider
> them rubbish, that I may gain Christ.
> —PHILIPPIANS 3:8

I cry to God every day asking the Lord to destroy any type
of stronghold that discourages the church from carrying out
the Great Commission that God gave. I ask God to give them
victory over fear of the Muslims.

GOD IS MOVING

There are Christians in the Middle East who do not follow
the typical pattern. They are working hard and courageously
to give the Good News to any type of person they
encounter. These are wonderful people, and my prayer is
for more of them.

I salute the courage of people like Pastor A.B., a young
man of thirty who is living in Cairo. He was raised in the
evangelical church in Egypt. He is working underground
amongst the Muslims there, telling them about the Good
News. I met him during a lecture at a Christian college. He
was full of love for all people without Jesus. He told me, "I
believe that our responsibility as God's children is to evangelize the Jews in the Middle East and to witness to them and
tell them about the Messiah."

This is the desire of my heart. It is my cry to God that He
can put His love in the Middle Eastern church for Jews and
also for Muslims. I pray that the church can be a bridge
between Muslims and Jews in the Middle East. I ask the Lord
to change their hearts and give them a better understanding
of the Word of God and the heart of Jesus Christ.

The Lord is faithful, and He can answer our prayer. The Lord is more jealous than me—more than anyone—for His church. He has a plan for His church, and He will fulfill that plan.

The Spirit of God is moving every day in the hearts of the Christians and Christian leaders in the Middle East. The Lord is opening the eyes of His children, and they are seeing the heart of God toward Jews and Muslims.

CHAPTER 26

Testimonies From the PLO and Hizbollah

N O ONE IS BEYOND JESUS' ABILITY to change. Here I would like to tell you the stories of two former Muslims. The first is a man who was doing combat against Israel with the PLO. The second is a woman who was doing weapons training for Hizbollah, a radical Islamic group in Lebanon.

FORMER PLO MEMBER TAKES GOSPEL TO JEWS

This is the wonderful testimony of a Palestinian man who grew up in Saudi Arabia and fought for the PLO (Palestinian Liberation Organization). He told me:

> After the Six-Day War in 1967, I decided to leave Saudi Arabia and join the Palestinian Liberation Organization in Jordan to fight and to kill the Jews. I was stationed at the border of Jordan and Israel.
>
> I fought in many battles between the PLO and the Israelis in the 1960s and 1970s. I remembered that one day I was sitting with two of my friends with whom I fought when suddenly an Israeli bomb hit in the midst of us, and both my friends were blown in half right in front of me. They died immediately. I went to the hospital, and I found out that I wasn't injured at all.
>
> In 1974, I left Jordan and returned to the Gulf countries. My family asked me to travel to Egypt to continue my studies. But I told them that I wished to continue

my studies in America, not in Egypt. My family became very upset and said, "That isn't possible. We cannot send you there. It's the country of the Great Satan."

After I caused lots of trouble to my family, they allowed me to travel to the United States. I arrived there, and I went to study at a university.

I met an American Christian believer who started to evangelize me, telling me about Jesus. At first I rejected the idea that Jesus could be a savior. I also rejected the idea that Jesus could be the Son of God. But this American Christian started to take me to the Book of John, explaining to me about the truth of Jesus Christ, the Savior, who is the Son of God.

Later on, the Lord touched my heart and saved me. I felt as if there were a mountain on my back that was taken away when I came to the Lord. I started to experience the peace and the comfort of Jesus Christ over my life.

The Word of God through the Bible came to me in a very simple way. I learned that God said, "Love one another and love your enemies." The first people that the Lord had put on my heart were the Jews, the people I had fought against. After I was saved, I started praying for the Jews. Many times I asked myself, *Why did I hate these people like that? Why had I declared them my enemies and gone out and killed them?*

I realized that I had lived my life by the deception of the Islamic belief and culture.

This man's life was changed dramatically. He now shares the love of Jesus Christ with the Jewish community in the United States. The Lord is using him in an amazing way.

It is nothing short of a miracle that a Palestinian Muslim, who was killing Jews and who was on the payroll of the Palestinian Liberation Organization, found true liberation from the only true Liberator, Jesus Christ. Now, instead of being in the army of Yasser Arafat, he is in God's army, not to bring the lives of Jews to an end, but to give the lives of Jews a new beginning.

MEMBER OF HIZBOLLAH MEETS JESUS THROUGH MESSIANIC JEW

During my visit to the state of Michigan three years ago, I met a Muslim woman from Lebanon who had accepted Jesus. From the first moment I spoke with her, I felt there was a heavy story in this woman's past. I was interested to find out more about her life before she came to the United States. The Lord answered my prayer, and I recently interviewed her. Here is her story.

In 1967, after the Six-Day War, and after the black July when the Jordanian king was killing thousands of Palestinians in Jordan, I felt that I had to stand with the Palestinians and do whatever I could. I started to collect food and clothes in and around where I lived, and I put them in a container, taking it to the Palestinian refugees. The picture was starting to become clear more and more about the conflict in the Middle East between the Arab Muslims and the Jews.

I started to believe that Israel had no right to exist in the Middle East because the land was a Muslim one. I believed that it was not promised for the Jews. I was taught it should be an Islamic state and a Palestinian nation there—not Israel, not for the Jews.

In 1975, after the death of my father, I decided to join the Muslim militant group fighting the Israelis in South Lebanon [Hizbollah]. I became a trainer, training the young people how to use the weapons [guns, rockets] and how to fight the Jews in South Lebanon.

I lived for five years after my father's death struggling with the ideology and teaching of Islam. During these years of struggling I harbored great anger and hatred, not only toward the Jews, but also toward the Arab countries that acted so weak and forgot their responsibility to stand in the face of the Jews and to fight them and to liberate Palestine from the Jewish hands.

My disappointment with Arabs and the Arabic countries was always making me question, "Allah, Where are you?"

When I started reading the Quran, I realized that this problem wasn't just between Muslims and Jews; it was between Allah and the Jews first. In the midst of this situation, I started to ask myself whether Allah were on the side of the Jews, because the Jews never stopped beating the Arabs when they fought with one another. In 1948, 1956, 1967, 1973—in all these wars the Jews were always victorious. So if there were a God who cared for them to help them win, it must be a different God from the one I knew. I started searching for this God.

My father had been desirous of me to leave Lebanon and go to the United States to have a peaceful and stable life. Several years after his death, I felt I had to be faithful to him and leave the Middle East to live in the United States.

The Lord did a miracle in my life when I came to the United States. I visited an American church, and there I met a Jewish woman who had accepted the Lord Jesus. She worshiped in this church. We started a friendship, and she shared Jesus with me. Through her the Lord delivered me from Islam and drew me into His kingdom and His family.

The most exciting thing about God's plan for my life was that He used a Jewish woman to tell me about Jesus and to lead me to Him. The Lord destroyed every wall between me and the Jews. The Lord destroyed the stronghold of Islam and the hatred that I grew up with toward the Jews. He united me with this Jewish woman to be sisters in the blood of Jesus Christ.

Before I was saved, I believed that Jerusalem would be delivered from the hands of the Jews and returned to the Muslims. All my prayers to Allah were for him to be with the Muslims and give them victory over the Jewish nation. After I got saved, the stronghold of racism against non-Muslims, especially the Jews, fell down in a pile of ashes. Today I do not pray for one nation—I pray for the entire world, including Muslims and Jews, to come to the knowledge of Jesus Christ. I believe there isn't anyone who can reconcile the Muslim and the Jew except Jesus. He is the only one who can establish peace in the Middle East through both Jews and Muslims accepting Him and being redeemed by His blood.

CONCLUSION

I believe we will hear more testimonies like these as God moves among Muslim people. The events of September 11, 2001 have had a positive effect on Muslim evangelism. That day showed the whole world, including Muslims, how ugly Islam is. By my estimation, more Muslims were converted to Christianity in the year after September 11 than have been converted in the past two hundred years.

Epilogue

THE SUBTITLE OF THIS BOOK IS "The Unfinished Battle." This refers to Islam's unfinished battle against the Jews. However, there are other levels of meaning as well.

First, Satan is fighting an unfinished battle against God. Satan's goal is to prevent as many people as possible from knowing God, and he has done this successfully with 1.3 billion people who are following Islam.

Second, the Christian church is fighting an unfinished battle to bring the Good News to all the people of the world, including the Muslims and the Jews. This is not a fight in the natural world. This is a fight in the spiritual world that must be supported by prayer.

Please join with me in prayer.

PRAYER FOR MUSLIMS

Ask God to break down the stronghold and the influence of the following:

1. The power of the Quran over Muslims
2. The power of the prayers that Muslims pray five times a day
3. The power of Ramadan month (the month of fasting)
4. The power of Muslim mosques and Muslim preaching
5. The power of Mecca, specifically the pilgrimage (*hajj*)
6. The power of the Arab/Muslim culture
7. The power of the world media, who create an opportunity for the poison of Islam to spread

worldwide and deceive many

8. The power of Muhammad's name, personality and way of life over Muslims, because he is the example they follow. We want God to destroy this example in their lives and replace it with Jesus.

9. The spirit of religion that has captured millions of people in the Middle East and around the Islamic world

10. The historical stronghold of hatred in Muslims' hearts toward Jews

11. Pray for new revelation from God to Muslim peoples so that they can see the true Jesus of the Bible, not the false one presented in the Quran.

12. Pray for a breakthrough in reaching out to Muslims worldwide, specifically in the Islamic countries, breaking the spirit of antichrist among government leaders who make laws that prohibit Christian missionary activity.

13. Pray for clear vision and good strategy for reaching Muslims worldwide.

14. Pray for Muslims to experience the love of Jesus.

PRAYER FOR CHRISTIANS

1. Ask the Lord to challenge the Christian church to love the Muslim converts and to adopt them into the body of Jesus Christ.

2. Pray for God to raise up workers to reach out to Muslims.

3. Pray for God to provide the finances and equipment for the missionaries who are going to work in the Middle East.

4. Pray that God will bring together Muslim converts and Messianic Jews so that they can work together to bring salvation to both Muslims and Jews.

5. Pray for the Spirit of God to reveal Himself supernaturally to people who are influenced by the spirit of religion and to show them the nature of His character.

PRAYER FOR THE AUTHOR

May I also ask you to remember me in your prayers.

1. Pray for me as a Christian soldier standing on the front lines, proclaiming the name of Jesus against the spirit of Islam, working and crying for Muslims to come and to see the light of Jesus.

2. Pray for my protection from the evil of Islam and safety for my travels.

3. Pray for my family, that the Lord can shine His light upon their lives and bring them to the knowledge of Jesus Christ.

4. Pray for the team that I am working with in this great ministry for protection and blessing from the Lord.

APPENDIX A

Abraham and Ishmael: Who Tells the Real Story?

T O GET TO THE TRUTH, YOU have to do some digging. Reading this essay will take some extra effort on your part, but the reward will be a very deep understanding of what Islam teaches about Abraham and his two sons, Ishmael and Isaac. This will take you a long way toward understanding the relationship between Muslims and Jews today.

THE SIGNIFICANCE OF ABRAHAM AND ISHMAEL TO A MUSLIM

To a Muslim, Abraham is the first true worshiper of Allah. Abraham is an example of submission to Allah because he rejected his own people to follow the one true god.

Muslims honor Ishmael as a great prophet on the same level as Moses to the Jews. They believe Allah commanded Abraham to take Ishmael, not Isaac, on the mountain to be sacrificed. Therefore, Ishmael is honored for his submission to Allah. When a Muslim takes a pilgrimage to Mecca, he must sacrifice a lamb in memory of Ishmael.[1]

The Quran refers to Allah several times as the god of Abraham, Ishmael, Isaac and Jacob (Surah 2:133; see also Surah 2:136, 140; 3:84; 4:163).

There are three significant events involving Abraham and Ishmael that are taught in Islam:

1. Abraham leaves Ishmael and his mother in the desert.
2. Abraham offers Ishmael as a sacrifice to Allah.
3. Abraham and Ishmael build a temple to Allah together.

In the next pages we will compare the Bible account and the Islamic account (based on the Quran and Muhammad's teachings). I will point out the significant differences between the two. I will also explain what these differences demonstrate, including that:

* Muhammad used the story of Abraham to make Islam more appealing to his audience.

* The Islamic account of events has logical inconsistencies.

* Muhammad's distortion of their Scriptures helped cause the Jews of Arabia to turn against him.

* The differences between the biblical and Islamic accounts are so great that one must be wrong and the other must be right.

ABRAHAM LEAVES HAGAR AND ISHMAEL IN THE DESERT

Ishmael was the son of Abraham and his wife's Egyptian servant Hagar. The conflict between Hagar and Abraham's wife Sarah became so bad that Abraham sent Hagar away. The Bible tells this story, as did Muhammad (in hadith). Now we will compare these two stories and see the false picture that is presented to Muslims.

Ishmael and Hagar: the Islamic version

Abraham took Hagar and Ishmael to Mecca, [which is

in present-day Saudi Arabia]. Hagar sat down to nurse Ishmael, and Abraham put a bag of dates and a water skin of water near them.[2]

Then Abraham started to travel back to his home. Abraham prayed for Hagar and Ishmael to receive favor and sustenance from the people they would encounter.*

Hagar's water ran out, and she could no longer nurse Ishmael. The child began tossing in agony, and she left him because she could not bear to look at him. Hagar was in a small valley, and she climbed the nearest mountain, called As-Safe. She looked for help and saw no one. So she ran across the valley to the mountain on the opposite side, called Al-Marwah. [These mountains are at present-day Mecca]. Again she looked for help. She repeated this seven times.

The last time she heard a voice and then saw an angel at the place of *Zamzam* [This is a spring that is in Mecca]. The angel dug at the earth with his heel (or wing) until the water flowed out. The angel told her: "Don't be afraid of being neglected, for this is the House of Allah, which will be built by this boy and his father, and Allah never neglects his people."[3]

When Muslims do the *hajj*, they have special duties in remembrance of this story. The Quran teaches:

> Verily! *As-Safa* and *Al-Marwah* (two mountains in Makkah) are of the Symbols of Allah. So it is not a sin on him who performs *Hajj* or *'Umrah* (pilgrimage) of the House (the *Ka'bah at Makkah*) to perform the going (*Tawaf*) between them (*As-Safa* and *Al-Marwa*).
> —SURAH 2:158

This tradition is still practiced today. When you go to Mecca

---

*This prayer is in Surah 14:37.

for *hajj*, you will go to a huge corridor that is built inside the mosque. The corridor has a divider in the middle. Thousands of people at a time move back and forth, back and forth through this great corridor to commemorate Hagar going back and forth between the mountains. Afterward the people crowd around the spring that Hagar was said to drink from.

When I made my own pilgrimage to Mecca as a Muslim, I was a part of this crowd of people. As a scholar, I understood the significance of what I was doing. But in my heart it felt very empty.

Now let's look at the biblical version of the story.

Ishmael and Hagar: the biblical version

> Sarah became angry when Ishmael, who was about sixteen years old at the time, was mocking during the great feast that was held when Isaac was weaned. Sarah insisted that Hagar and Ishmael be sent away. Abraham was distressed, but God told Abraham, "I will make the son of the maidservant into a nation also, because he is your offspring."
>
> The next morning Abraham took some food and water and gave them to Hagar. Then he sent her and Ishmael away, and they wandered into the desert of Beersheba. [This is the present-day Sinai Desert in Egypt, which is close to Canaan, but a long way from Mecca.]
>
> When the water was gone, Hagar put Ishmael under a bush and went away because she could not bear to watch him die. God heard Ishmael crying and the angel of God called to Hagar and said, "Do not be afraid... for I will make him into a great nation."
>
> Then God opened Hagar's eyes, and she saw a well of water. She filled the skin with water and gave it to Ishmael.
>
> —GENESIS 21:8–19, AUTHOR'S PARAPHRASE

Important differences

Where was Abraham living with Hagar, Sarah and the two sons?

✴ Hadith/Quran: Not clear
✴ Bible: Canaan (in the area of present-day Israel)

Where did Hagar go?

✴ Hadith/Quran: Abraham took her to Mecca
✴ Bible: Abraham sent her away, and she wandered to the Sinai Desert.

How old was Ishmael when Abraham sent him and his mother away?

✴ Hadith/Quran: a nursing child, probably two years old or less
✴ Bible: Sixteen years old

Let's consider where Abraham and his family were living. The Bible says they were in Canaan. On the other hand, if you study Islamic history only, you will get the impression that Abraham stayed in Chaldea. (Islamic history makes no mention of him going to Canaan.) Please refer to the map on page 198 and see how far Abraham, Hagar and the infant/toddler Ishmael had to travel to get to Mecca from Chaldea. If they had the benefit of traveling by camel, it would have taken three months or more. By car today it would take around thirty hours.

Now consider the biblical account. See how close the Sinai Desert is to Canaan. It is easy to see how a woman and a sixteen-year-old boy could walk there. By camel it would take less than one week. You can get there by car one day.

What promise did God make about Ishmael?

✴ Hadith: He and his father would build the House of Allah in Mecca.

Abraham's Journeys

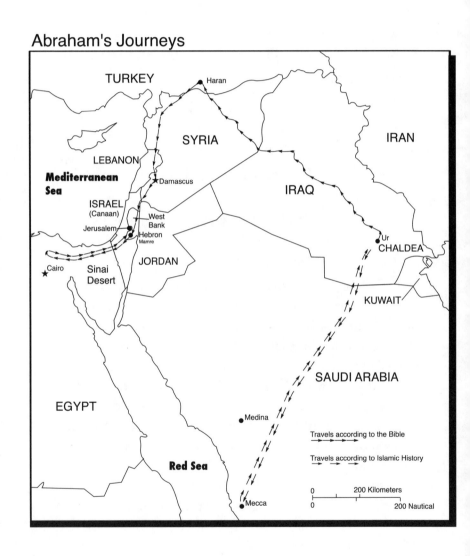

* Bible: The descendants of Ishmael will be a great nation.

Remember that the Arabs recognized Ishmael as their father. Consider the benefits to Muhammad of having Ishmael build a place of worship in Mecca. This would help open the Arab's hearts to his message. It also used their established respect for the Kaaba, the temple where the tribes worshiped their own idols in Mecca already.

ABRAHAM SACRIFICING HIS SON

Abraham offers his son: the Quranic version

So We gave him the glad tidings of a forbearing boy.[4] And, when he (his son) was old enough to walk with him, he said: "O my son! I have seen in a dream that I am slaughtering you (offering you in sacrifice to Allah). So look what you think!" He said: "O my father! Do that which you are commanded, *Insha Allah* (if Allah wills), you shall find me of *As-Sabirun* (the patient).

Then, when they had both submitted themselves (to the Will of Allah), and he had laid him prostrate on his forehead (or on the side of his forehead for slaughtering); We called out to him: "O Abraham! You have fulfilled the dream!"

Verily thus do We reward the *Husinun* (good-doers—See 2:112). Verily, that indeed was a manifest trial. And We ransomed him with a great sacrifice (i.e., a ram); and we left for him (a goodly remembrance) among the later generations.

—SURAH 37:101–108

The Quran didn't say the name of the son—Isaac or Ishmael, but the Muslims believe it is Ishmael. Muslim commentaries on the Quran consistently interpret this to refer to Ishmael. Isaac is the father of the Jews, so he would not be spoken of with honor in Muslim scriptures. Also, the Quran says that Abraham and Ishmael built the House of Allah in Mecca together. That's why Muslims are sure this passage refers to Ishmael. In Muslim minds, the story of Abraham is revolving around Ishmael.

Abraham offers his son: the biblical version

Abraham took the wood for the burnt offering and placed it on his son Isaac, and he himself carried the fire and the knife. As the two of them went on together, Isaac spoke up and said to his father Abraham, "Father?"

"Yes, my son?" Abraham replied.

"The fire and wood are here," Isaac said, "but where is the lamb for the burnt offering?"

Abraham answered, "God himself will provide the lamb for the burnt offering, my son." And the two of them went on together.

When they reached the place God had told him about, Abraham built an altar there and arranged the wood on it. He bound his son Isaac and laid him on the altar, on top of the wood. Then he reached out his hand and took the knife to slay his son. But the angel of the Lord called out to him from heaven, "Abraham! Abraham!"

"Here I am," he replied.

"Do not lay a hand on the boy," he said. "Do not do anything to him. Now I know that you fear God, because you have not withheld from me your son, your only son."

Abraham looked up and there in a thicket he saw a ram caught by its horns. He went over and took the ram and sacrificed it as a burnt offering instead of his son. So Abraham called that place The LORD Will Provide. And to this day it is said, "On the mountain of the Lord it will be provided."

—GENESIS 22:6–14

Important differences

The biblical record is clear that the child is Isaac. The Quran does not say the name of the child. I think this was deliberate. Muhammad could not say Ishmael at the time of the revelation because he and his followers were a weak group living in Mecca. But later Muhammad made bold statements about Ishmael.

Another challenge to the validity of the Quranic story is the fact that Ishmael was not living with Abraham's family as a young boy. Remember that Ishmael (according to Islam) was an infant/toddler when Abraham sent Hagar away. The age of the child in the sacrifice story is said to be about nine.[5] So how did Abraham restore contact with Ishmael in order to offer him as a sacrifice? Did Abraham travel all the way from Chaldea to Mecca for this one event?

Do you see how Islam's differences from the biblical record cause other inconsistencies? If the facts about one thing are changed, it affects the validity of the whole system.

ISHMAEL GROWING UP

The Islamic story of Ishmael continued to be different from the biblical account. The hadith says that Hagar and Ishmael settled in Mecca around the spring that the angel dug. When other tribes saw that they had water, they joined them there. The hadith said that Ishmael's first wife came from one of these tribes.

In contrast, the Bible says:

> God was with the boy as he grew up. He lived in the desert [the Sinai Desert next to Canaan] and became an archer. While he was living in the Desert of Paran, his mother got a wife for him from Egypt.
>
> —GENESIS 21:20–21

After Ishmael was grown and married, he went to Mecca. He died there.*

The differences

Again Muhammad made up different details in the life of Ishmael in order to sustain the new version of history presented in Islam.

ABRAHAM AND ISHMAEL BUILDING
A TEMPLE/ALTAR FOR GOD

According to Islamic teaching, one of the most important events in the life of Abraham was working with Ishmael to build a house for God in Mecca.

> And (remember) when Ibrahim (Abraham) and (his son) Ismail (Ishmael) were raising the foundations of the House (the *Ka'bah* at Makkah), (saying), "Our Lord! Accept (this service) from us. Verily! You are the All-Hearer, the All-Knower."
>
> —SURAH 2:127

In the verse above from the Quran, it mentions that Abraham, with the help of his son Ishmael, built a house of God in the city of Mecca in Arabia. Muhammad also told the story in more detail in hadith. After Abraham came to Mecca and found Ishmael:

> Ibrahim (Abraham) said, "O Ismail (Ishmael)! Allah has given me an order." Ismail (Ishmael) said, "Do what your Lord has ordered you to do." Ibrahim (Abraham) asked, "Will you help me?" Ismail (Ishmael) said, "I will help you." Ibrahim (Abraham) said, "Allah has ordered me to build a house here," pointing to a hillock higher than the land surrounding it.

---

* The Bible doesn't say where Ishmael died, but there is reason to believe it really was Mecca.

Muhammad said the two of them made a foundation and then built the walls of stone, Ishmael bringing stones and Abraham building. When the walls became high, Ishmael brought a big stone for Abraham to stand on, and they continued to work.[6]

We see today a big mosque in Mecca, and in the midst of this mosque, there is a big, black stone. According to Islam, this is the most holy site in the world.

During *hajj* every year, millions of Muslims come to this mosque and walk around the black stone and visit what Muslims believe to be the grave of Abraham that is nearby. When I went on *hajj*, I too circled the black stone with this great mass of people.

Muslims never question that Abraham was the builder of Kaaba or that he lived with Ishmael in Mecca after building the mosque and then died and was buried there. No Scripture in the Bible says Abraham did these things. Instead the Bible presents a different set of facts. (See the Summary of the Travels of Abraham on page 204.)

According to the Bible, Abraham emigrated from Chaldea (now in southern Iraq) to Haran (at the border of Turkey and Syria). Then he moved to Canaan (which is in Israel today). All of the travels of Abraham after he settled in Canaan were between Canaan and Egypt. (See Genesis 12:7–10; 13:18.) He built altars but no temples. He died and was buried in a cave near Mamre (Gen. 25:9–10). See the map on page 198.

EXPOSING LIES

When it comes to the revelations about the life of Abraham and Ishmael, the Bible and the Quran/hadith cannot be reconciled. In other words, one source must be true and the other false. They cannot both be true.

Summary of the Travels of Abraham

Islamic history

Abraham was born in Ur of the Chaldeans, but there was no record regarding where he and his wives lived. Islamic history implies that he stayed in Chaldea. Abraham made five trips to Mecca:

1. Abraham took Hagar and the baby Ishmael to Mecca and left them there.

2. Abraham took Ishmael to be sacrificed on a mountain near Mecca.

3. Abraham visited Ishmael's home in Mecca and spoke to his first wife.

4. Abraham visited Ishmael's home in Mecca and spoke to his second wife.

5. Abraham went to Ishmael, and they built the House of God (al-Kaaba) in Mecca together. Abraham remained in Mecca until his death and was buried there.

The Bible account

Abraham was born in Ur of the Chaldeans but went to Canaan and settled there with his family. He sent Hagar and Ishmael away to the Sinai Desert when Ishmael was sixteen years old, but Abraham did not travel with them. Abraham made some trips back and forth to Egypt. Abraham died in Canaan and was buried at Mamre near Hebron.

The point I want to make is that it is not acceptable for Muhammad to claim that he had new information about events that were on record for thousands of years. It is not right for him to claim that the biblical record was corrupted, making it necessary for the true version (the Quran) to be revealed. It is not right to say the original biblical record would be consistent with the Quran if the Christians and Jews had not changed it. There is no evidence that Christians and Jews changed their Scriptures. There are no archeological findings. There are no copies of the original manuscripts from the Torah or from the New Testament. The New Testament was only six hundred years earlier. Surely one copy of the original manuscripts would have been found to show as proof of what Muhammad said.

How can we learn something new from the time of Abraham? God is not going to reveal a new story. He told the truth the first time, and the Jews preserved it accurately. The only way to discover something in addition to the biblical record is by archeology. If we in modern times dig up something from the time of Abraham and study it, then perhaps we can add to our body of information. Other than direct evidence, there is no way to learn something new—not now and not in seventh-century Arabia.

Let me be perfectly clear on this point: The Bible and the Quran do not agree. One is right, and one is wrong.

IF ISHMAEL WERE SO SPECIAL, WHY DID GOD USE JACOB AT ALL?

Now you can see for yourself the way of the Bible and the way of Islam in teaching about Abraham and Ishmael. There is one last problem I would like to point out with the Islamic teaching.

First, remember Muhammad said the descendants from

the line of Isaac and Jacob (i.e., the Jews) were God's chosen people. They were the source of all the prophets and keepers of the revelation in the Torah.

But Muhammad also said that Ishmael was a special son, building the temple with his father, Abraham, and being the son who submitted to sacrifice.

So here's the question, *If* Ishmael were the special, chosen son, why did God use the line of Isaac and Jacob at all? Why didn't God just send all his prophets through the line of Ishmael?

If you ask a Muslim scholar these questions, he will struggle to answer. He will probably say, "It was Allah's will. Yes, the prophets came from Jacob's line, but Jacob and Ishmael are brothers in Islam. All the children of Abraham came to preach the same message."

In reality, this inconsistency shows again that Allah, the god of Islam, could not be the same as the God of the Jews and the Christians. If they were the same god, then he is a god of disorganization and confusion.

CONCLUSION

The story of Abraham and Ishmael is just one of many examples of Muhammad and the Quran using Old Testament teachings. I hope this comparison has helped you see how the relationship between Muhammad and the Jews of Arabia broke down as Muhammad distorted their Scriptures and used these teachings to put down the Jewish people.

APPENDIX B

Osama bin Laden: Jihad Against Jews and Crusaders

THIS APPENDIX SHOWS THE TEXT OF the World Islamic Front Statement urging jihad against Jews and Crusaders.[1]

> FAS Note: The following statement from Usama bin Laden and his associates purports to be a religious ruling (fatwa) requiring the killing of Americans, both civilian and military. This document is part of the evidence that links the bin Laden network to the September 11 terrorist attacks on New York and Washington.

> **Jihad Against Jews and Crusaders**
> **World Islamic Front Statement**
> **23 February 1998**

* Shaykh Usamah Bin-Muhammad Bin-Ladin

* Ayman al-Zawahiri, amir of the Jihad Group in Egypt

* Abu-Yasir Rifa'i Ahmad Taha, Egyptian Islamic Group

* Shaykh Mir Hamzah, secretary of the Jamiat-ul-Ulema-e-Pakistan

* Fazlur Rahman, amir of the Jihad Movement in Bangladesh.

Praise be to Allah, who revealed the Book, controls the clouds, defeats factionalism, and says in His Book: "But when the forbidden months are past, then fight and slay the pagans wherever ye find them, seize them, beleaguer them, and lie in wait for them in every stratagem (of war)"; and peace be upon our Prophet, Muhammad Bin-'Abdullah, who said: I have been sent with the sword between my hands to ensure that no one but Allah is worshiped, Allah who put my livelihood under the shadow of my spear and who inflicts humiliation and scorn on those who disobey my orders.

The Arabian Peninsula has never—since Allah made it flat, created its desert, and encircled it with seas—been stormed by any forces like the crusader armies spreading in it like locusts, eating its riches and wiping out its plantations. All this is happening at a time in which nations are attacking Muslims like people fighting over a plate of food. In the light of the grave situation and the lack of support, we and you are obliged to discuss current events, and we should all agree on how to settle the matter.

No one argues today about three facts that are known to everyone; we will list them, in order to remind everyone:

> First, for over seven years the United States has been occupying the lands of Islam in the holiest of places, the Arabian Peninsula, plundering its riches, dictating to its rulers, humiliating its people, terrorizing its neighbors, and turning its bases in the Peninsula into a spearhead through which to fight the neighboring Muslim peoples.

> If some people have in the past argued

about the fact of the occupation, all the people of the Peninsula have now acknowledged it. The best proof of this is the Americans' continuing aggression against the Iraqi people using the Peninsula as a staging post, even though all its rulers are against their territories being used to that end, but they are helpless.

Second, despite the great devastation inflicted on the Iraqi people by the crusader-Zionist alliance, and despite the huge number of those killed, which has exceeded 1 million... despite all this, the Americans are once against [*sic*] trying to repeat the horrific massacres, as though they are not content with the protracted blockade imposed after the ferocious war or the fragmentation and devastation.

So here they come to annihilate what is left of this people and to humiliate their Muslim neighbors.

Third, if the Americans' aims behind these wars are religious and economic, the aim is also to serve the Jews' petty state and divert attention from its occupation of Jerusalem and murder of Muslims there. The best proof of this is their eagerness to destroy Iraq, the strongest neighboring Arab state, and their endeavor to fragment all the states of the region such as Iraq, Saudi Arabia, Egypt, and Sudan into paper statelets and through their disunion and weakness to guarantee Israel's survival and the continuation of the brutal crusade occupation of the Peninsula.

All these crimes and sins committed by the Americans are a clear declaration of war on Allah, his messenger, and Muslims. And ulema have throughout Islamic history unanimously agreed that the jihad is an individual duty if the enemy destroys the Muslim countries. This was revealed by Imam Bin-Qadamah in "Al- Mughni," Imam al-Kisa'i in "Al-Bada'i," al-Qurtubi in his interpretation, and the shaykh of al-Islam in his books, where he said: "As for the fighting to repulse [an enemy], it is aimed at defending sanctity and religion, and it is a duty as agreed [by the ulema]. Nothing is more sacred than belief except repulsing an enemy who is attacking religion and life."

On that basis, and in compliance with Allah's order, we issue the following fatwa to all Muslims:

The ruling to kill the Americans and their allies— civilians and military—is an individual duty for every Muslim who can do it in any country in which it is pos-sible to do it, in order to liberate the al-Aqsa Mosque [on the Temple Mount in Jerusalem] and the holy mosque [in Mecca] from their grip, and in order for their armies to move out of all the lands of Islam, defeated and unable to threaten any Muslim. This is in accordance with the words of Almighty Allah, "and fight the pagans all together as they fight you all together," and "fight them until there is no more tumult or oppression, and there prevail justice and faith in Allah."

This is in addition to the words of Almighty Allah: "And why should ye not fight in the cause of Allah and of those who, being weak, are ill-treated (and oppressed)?— women and children, whose cry is: 'Our Lord, rescue us from this town, whose people are oppressors; and raise for us from thee one who will help!'"

We—with Allah's help—call on every Muslim who believes in Allah and wishes to be rewarded to comply with Allah's order to kill the Americans and plunder their money wherever and whenever they find it. We also call on Muslim ulema, leaders, youths, and soldiers to launch the raid on Satan's U.S. troops and the devil's supporters allying with them, and to displace those who are behind them so that they may learn a lesson.

Almighty Allah said: "O ye who believe, give your response to Allah and His Apostle, when He calleth you to that which will give you life. And know that Allah cometh between a man and his heart, and that it is He to whom ye shall all be gathered."

Almighty Allah also says: "O ye who believe, what is the matter with you, that when ye are asked to go forth in the cause of Allah, ye cling so heavily to the earth! Do ye prefer the life of this world to the hereafter? But little is the comfort of this life, as compared with the hereafter. Unless ye go forth, He will punish you with a grievous penalty, and put others in your place; but Him ye would not harm in the least. For Allah hath power over all things."

Almighty Allah also says: "So lose no heart, nor fall into despair. For ye must gain mastery if ye are true in faith."

On page 212 is the Arabic version of *fatwa* above:[2]

نص بيان الجبهة الاسلامية العالمية لجهاد اليهود والصليبيين

الحمد لله منزل الكتاب ومجري السحاب، وهازم الأحزاب، والقائل في محكم كتابه «فإذا انسلخ الأشهر الحرم، فاقتلوا المشركين حيث وجدتموهم، وخذوهم واحصروهم، واقعدوا لهم كل مرصد» والصلاة والسلام على نبينا محمد بن عبد الله، القائل «بعثت بالسيف بين يدي الساعة حتى يعبد الله وحده لا شريك له، وجعل رزقي تحت ظل رمحي، وجعل الذل والصغار على من خالف أمري».

أما بعد

فمنذ أن دحى الله جزيرة العرب، وخلق فيها صحراءها، وحفها ببحارها لم تدهمها غاشية كهذه القوات الصليبية التي انتشرت فيها كالجراد تزحم في أرضها وتأكل ثرواتها، وتبيد خضراءها، كل ذلك في وقت تداعت فيه على المسلمين الأمم كما تداعت الأكلة الى قصعتها، ويزعجنا حين عظم الخطب، وقل الناصرين أن نظفر بأيكم على مكنون الأحداث الجارية، كما يجب أن نشفق جميعا على فصيل القضاء فيها.

لا أحد يجادل اليوم في حقائق ثلاث توارثت عليها الشواهد وأطبق عليها المسلمون ونحن نذكرها ليتذكر من يتذكر، ولنهلك من هلك عن بينة، ويحيا من حيا عن بينة وهم:

أولا منذ ما يربو عن نسبع سنين وامريكا تحتل اراضي الاسلام في اقدس بقاعها، جزيرة العرب، وتنهب خيراتها، وتملي على حكامها وتذل اهلها، وترعب جيرانها، وتجعل من قواعدها في الجزيرة رأس حربة تقاتل بها شعوب الاسلام المجاورة.

وإذا كان في الماضي من يجادل في حقيقة هذا الاحتلال فقد أطبق على الاعتراف به اهل الجزيرة جميعا.

ولا أدل على ذلك من تمادي الأمريكان في العدوان ضد شعب العراق انطلاقا من الجزيرة، رغم كل أهلها جميعا يرفضون استخدام ارضهم لذلك، ولكنهم مقهورون.

ثانيا رغم الدمار الكبير الذي حل بالشعب العراقي على يدي التحالف الصليبي اليهودي، ورغم العدد الفظيع من القتل الذي جاوز المليون، رغم كل ذلك يحاول الامريكان مرة اخرى معاودة هذه المجازر المروعة، وكأنهم لم يكتفوا بالحصار الطويل بعد الحرب العنيفة ولا بالتمزيق والتدمير.

فها هم يأتون اليوم ليبيدوا بقية هذا الشعب، وليذلوا جيرانه من المسلمين.

ثالثا، واذا كانت اهداف الامريكان من هذه الحروب دينية واقتصادية فانها كذلك تأتي لخدمة دويلة اليهود، ولصرف النظر عن احتلالها لبيت المقدس وقتلها للمسلمين فيه.

ولا أدل على ذلك من حرصهم على تدمير العراق قوى الدول العربية المجاورة، وسعيهم لتمزيق دول المنطقة جميعا كالعراق والسعودية ومصر

والسودان الى دويلات ورقية تضمن بفرقتها وضعفها بقاء اسرائيل واستمرار الاحتلال الصليبي الغاشم لارض الجزيرة.

ان كل تلك الجرائم والبوائق هي من الامريكان اعلان صريح للحرب على الله ورسوله وعلى المسلمين، وقد أجمع العلماء سلفا وخلفا عبر جميع العصور الاسلامية على أن الجهاد اذا دهم العدو بلاد المسلمين فرض عين، ومن نقل ذلك الامام ابن قدامة في «المغني» والامام الكساني في «البدائع» والقرطبي في تفسيره، وشيخ الاسلام في اختياراته، حيث قال: «اما قتال الدفع فهو اشد انواع دفع الصائل عن الحرمة والدين واجب اجماعا، فالعدو الصائل الذي يفسد الدين والدنيا لا شيء اوجب بعد الايمان من دفعه».

ونحن بناء على ذلك وامتثالا لأمر الله نفتي جميع المسلمين بالحكم التالي:

ان حكم قتل الامريكان وحلفائهم مدنيين وعسكريين فرض عين على كل مسلم امكنه ذلك في كل بلد تيسر فيه، وذلك حتى يتحرر المسجد الأقصى والمسجد الحرام من قبضتهم، وحتى تخرج جيوشهم عن كل أرض الاسلام مثلولة الحد كسيرة الجناح عاجزة عن تهديد أي مسلم، امتثالا لقوله تعالى «وقاتلوا المشركين كافة كما يقاتلونكم كافة»، وقوله تعالى «وقاتلوهم حتى لا تكون فتنة ويكون الدين لله».

وقوله تعالى «وما لكم لا تقاتلون في سبيل الله والمستضعفين من النساء والولدان الذين يقولون ربنا أخرجنا من هذه القرية الظالم اهلها واجعل لنا من لدنك وليا واجعل لنا من لدنك نصيرا».

اننا بإذن الله ندعو كل مسلم يؤمن بالله ويرغب في ثواب الله الى امتثال امر الله بقتل الامريكان ونهب اموالهم في أي مكان وجدهم فيه، وفي أي وقت امكنه ذلك، كما ندعو علماء المسلمين وقادتهم وشبابهم وجنودهم شن الغارة على جنود أب ليس الامريكان، ومن تحالف معهم من اعوان الشيطان.

وأن يشردوا بهم من خلفهم لعلهم يذكرون.

وقال الله تعالى «يا أيها الذين آمنوا استجيبوا لله وللرسول اذا دعاكم لما يحييكم».

واعلموا ان الله يحول بين المرء وقلبه وانه اليه تحشرون.

وقوله تعالى: «يا أيها الذين آمنوا ما لكم اذا قيل لكم انفروا في سبيل الله اثاقلتم الى الارض، ارضيتم بالحياة الدنيا من الآخرة فما متاع الحياة الدنيا في الآخرة الا قليل، الا تنفروا يعذبكم عذابا اليما ويستبدل قوما غيركم ولا تضروه شيئا، والله على كل شيء قدير».

وقال الله تعالى: «ولا تهنوا ولا تحزنوا وانتم الأعلون ان كنتم مؤمنين».

212

The Biblical Prophecies
Islam Claims for Muhammad

DID YOU KNOW THAT ACCORDING to the Quran, the coming of Muhammad was prophesied in the Bible?

> And verily, it (the Quran, and its revelation to Prophet Muhammad), is (announced) in the Scriptures [i.e. the Taurat (Torah) and the Injeel (Gospel) of the former people.
>
> —SURAH 26:196

So why don't we see these prophecies clearly? The Quran teaches that Jews and Christians changed almost all the parts of their Scriptures that spoke about Muhammad.

> They change the words from their (right) places and have abandoned a good part of the Message that was sent to them.
>
> —SURAH 5:13[1]

However, Muslim scholars say, "There exists in the *Taurat* (Torah) and the *Injeel* (Gospel), even after the original text has been distorted, clear prophecies indicating the coming of the Prophet Muhammad."

Let's look now at the Bible verses cited by these Muslim scholars. We will go chronologically through the Bible.[2]

THE PROPHET

In the following passage God is speaking to Moses:

> I will raise up for them a prophet like you from among
> their brothers; I will put my words in his mouth, and he
> will tell them everything I command him.
> —DEUTERONOMY 18:18

God was telling Moses that He would give the children of
Israel a prophet so that the people would not have to hear
His voice directly. This verse was fulfilled by the coming of
Jesus Christ.

THE CORNERSTONE

> The stone the builders rejected has become the capstone;
> the Lord has done this, and it is marvelous in our eyes.
> —PSALM 118:22–23

Jesus quoted this prophecy in Matthew 21:42–43, indicating that He was the fulfillment.

THE COMING LIGHT

> Here is my servant, whom I uphold, my chosen one in
> whom I delight; I will put my Spirit on him and he will
> bring justice to the nations. He will not shout or cry
> out, or raise his voice in the streets.
> —ISAIAH 42:1–2

> I, the LORD, have called you in righteousness; I will take
> hold of your hand. I will keep you and will make you to
> be a covenant for the people and a light for the
> Gentiles, to open eyes that are blind, and to free cap-
> tives from prison and to release from the dungeon
> those who sit in darkness.
> —ISAIAH 42:6–7

Again, Christians believe strongly this prophecy refers to Jesus, who lived six hundred years before Muhammad.[3]

HOLY ONE FROM MOUNT PARAN

God came from Teman, the Holy One from Mount Paran. His glory covered the heavens and his praise filled the earth.

—HABAKKUK 3:3

The part of this verse that Muslims focus on is "the Holy One from Mount Paran." Muslims say Mount Paran is at Mecca, which was the birthplace of Muhammad. But in reality, Mount Paran is not in Arabia; it is in the Sinai Desert. So this prophecy does not make reference to Muhammad's birthplace.

THE COUNSELOR

And I will ask the Father, and he will give you another Counselor to be with you forever—the Spirit of truth. The world cannot accept him, because it neither sees him nor knows him. But you know him, for he lives with you and will be in you.

—JOHN 14:16–17

Christians agree that this is a reference to the Holy Spirit living inside a Christian believer. In addition, this verse says several things that are not true about Muhammad. For example, it says the counselor would be with them "forever." Muhammad did not stay with his followers forever. He died. Also it says that the world could neither see or know him. But Muhammad was seen and known by many people. Finally, it says that the Counselor would live inside the people. Muhammad could not live inside anybody because he was not a spirit.

> But the Counselor, the Holy Spirit, whom the Father will send in my name, will teach you all things and will remind you of everything I have said to you.
>
> —JOHN 14:26

This verse clearly says that the Counselor is the Holy Spirit.

> But I tell you the truth: It is for your good that I am going away. Unless I go away, the Counselor will not come to you...
>
> —JOHN 16:7

Again, Jesus' prophecy of the Holy Spirit as the coming Comforter is taken to refer to Muhammad.

Remember, Jesus later said more about this prophecy. When He was being taken up to heaven, He said, "Do not leave Jerusalem, but wait for the gift my Father promised, which you have heard me speak about. For John baptized with water, but in a few days you will be baptized with the Holy Spirit" (Acts 1:4–5). Later that promise was fulfilled on the Day of Pentecost when they heard the sound of a violent wind, saw tongues of fire and were filled with the Holy Spirit (Acts 2:1–4).

CONCLUSION

These are all the Bible references that were cited in *The Noble Quran* as prophecies pertaining to Muhammad. As you can see for yourself, these prophecies had their fulfillment outside of Muhammad. This is another indication of the weakness of Islamic doctrine about the corruption of Scriptures.

From the Mosque to the Church

I WAS AN EXEMPLARY MUSLIM. WHEN I was five years old, my family helped me to start memorizing the Quran. I completed the job when I was twelve. From elementary schools to high school, I attended only Islamic schools, not the public schools of Egypt. After I graduated, I went to Al-Azhar University, which is the largest, most prestigious Islamic university in the world. There I earned my bachelor's, master's and doctorate degrees in Islamic history and culture. I worked as a traveling lecturer for the university and served as the imam of a mosque outside of Cairo, Egypt.

Though I understood Islam deeply, I began to question it. When the university found out, they fired me immediately. The Egyptian secret police arrested me that night and interrogated me with torture for a week. This was what I got for asking questions about Islam, so I turned my back on Islam at that point.

A year later a Christian lady gave me a Bible, and I met Jesus for the first time as I read a sermon of Jesus. I chose to follow Him that night, and I lived secretly as a Christian in Egypt for about a year.

Finally I got the courage to tell my father. By his reaction, I knew I had to leave Egypt. After a long trip, during which the Lord preserved my life several times, I made it to South Africa. Wonderful Christian brothers and sisters there helped me to grow in my Christian life, especially those with Youth With A Mission in Cape Town. This began the journey of cleansing my heart of hatred toward others, including the Jews. Now I look forward to every opportunity I have to meet with a Jew, one of God's chosen people.

During my six years in South Africa I spoke in churches and helped groups involved with Muslim evangelism. The Muslims in the area came to know me quite well, and they were very angry about what I was doing.

In 2000, Christian friends in America persuaded me to come to the United States under religious asylum. So this is where I minister now.

On the cover of this book you see the name Mark Gabriel. As you might imagine, this was not my Muslim name in Egypt. I wanted to change my Muslim name to a Christian name to reflect my new life.

By choosing the Lord Jesus Christ, I had to sacrifice my country, Egypt. I had to sacrifice my family, who wanted to kill me. I had to sacrifice my culture by moving from country to country. I had to sacrifice my job as a professor of Islam. It wasn't easy at all, but the decision was clear: If I have Jesus in my life, I have everything, but if I lose Jesus, I will lose everything.

> For what profit is it to a man if he gains the whole world, and loses his own soul?
> —MATTHEW 16:26, NKJV

> And everyone who has left houses or brothers or sisters or father or mother or wife or children or lands, for My name's sake, shall receive a hundredfold, and inherit eternal life.
> —MATTHEW 19:29, NKJV

Author's Academic Credentials

Dr. Gabriel's academic credentials in Islamic history include:

* Bachelor's, master's and doctorate degrees in Islamic history and culture from Al-Azhar University, Cairo, Egypt

* Graduating second in his class of six thousand students for his bachelor's degree. This ranking was based on a test to verify he had memorized the entire Quran and an oral exam in his subject area.

* One of the youngest lecturers ever hired at Al-Azhar University. He started lecturing after he finished his master's degree and was working to finish his doctorate.

* Traveling lecturer. Al-Azhar University sent him to countries around the Middle East as a lecturer in Islamic history.

Al-Azhar University is the most respected, authoritative Islamic university in the world. It has been in continuous operation for more than one thousand years.

In addition to his academic training, Dr. Gabriel had practical experience, serving as the imam at a mosque in the Cairo suburbs.

After Dr. Gabriel became a Christian, he wanted to have a Christian education. He completed:

* Discipleship Training School with Youth With A Mission in Cape Town, South Africa.

* Master's degree in world religion from Florida Christian University in Orlando, Florida.

* Doctorate degree in Christian education from Florida Christian University in Orlando, Florida.

He is founder and president of Hope for the Nations, a missions organization dedicated to bringing the Good News to the entire world, including Muslims and Jews.

Notes

Introduction

1. Karen Armstrong, *Islam: A Short History* (New York: Random House, 2002), 10.
2. Ibid., 21.
3. Ibid.
4. Michael Elliott, "Islam's Prophet Motive," *Time* (December 23, 2002): 76.

Chapter 3: My Missing Brother

1. There were no crocodiles in this part of the Nile because of a large dam upstream.
2. You may remember the sad story of the U.S. military accidentally attacking a wedding party in Afghanistan in 2002 because they saw weapons being fired. Firing guns is a typical way to celebrate in the Middle East, but apparently the military did not know that.

Chapter 5: How My Heart Changed

1. I really prefer to use the phrase "Messianic Jews" to refer to Jews who have accepted Jesus Christ. They haven't lost their Jewishness, so I don't like to say "ex-Jew." I'm an ex-Muslim, but I'm not an ex-Egyptian!

Chapter 6: The Foundation of Islam

1. Ibn Kathir, *The Quran Commentary*.
2. This verse gives an example of the way the word *We* appears in the Quran in reference to Allah. However, this is not meant to say Allah is plural. It is an Arabic semantic device that denotes the greatness and power of Allah.

Chapter 7: Islam's Relationship to Judaism and Christianity

1. Abraham and Ishmael are key figures in Islamic teaching.

However, the Quranic record of their lives is in contradiction to the Bible record. For Muslims, these contradictions are very important because they mean that one version is right and the other is wrong. To examine this issue for yourself, you can read Appendix A.

2. From the hadith of Al-Bukhari, vol. 4, hadith no. 735; quoted by *The Noble Quran* in the note to Surah 2:252.

3. One popular Islamic history book (written by a Westerner) claims: "It was probably during the *riddah* wars that Muslims began to assert that Muhammad had been the last and greatest of the prophets, a claim that is not made explicitly in the Quran..." (Armstrong, *Islam: A Short History*, 26.) This statement ignores Muhammad's words in hadith, or appears to say that they are not really his teachings. However, the contents of the hadith were recorded during Muhammad's lifetime and rigorously checked for authenticity. Muhammad believed he was the final prophet, and he said so. To claim otherwise would be like saying Jesus never claimed to be the Son of God. (See John 5:16–30.)

4. The information division of the Israeli Foreign Ministry reports: "Hamas raises funds through a complex network of organizations. While the majority of these outwardly claim to support religious or civic activities, this charity (*zakat*) is also awarded to operatives, the families of terrorists killed, and the terrorism apparatus. In effect, there is no distinction between Hamas' civic and terrorist activities." (Information Division, Israel Foreign Ministry: www.israel-mfa.gov.il)

5. Islam says that works will earn you entrance into Paradise. In contrast, Jesus said faith and nothing else is required for admission into heaven. In Christianity, doing good works is a way of pleasing God and showing gratitude, but the works themselves do not earn entrance into heaven.

CHAPTER 8: DOES THE QURAN CALL FOR TOLERANCE OR HOLY WAR?

1. I would like to point out that you can find verses in the Quran that say, "Tolerate your enemy." But you will never

find a verse that says, "Love your enemies," as Jesus did (Matt. 5:44).

CHAPTER 9: THE "NICE ISLAM" OF THE WEST

1. One popular history book says, "The Quran does not sanctify warfare. It develops the notion of a just war of self-defense to protect decent values, but condemns killing and aggression." (Armstrong, *Islam: A Short History*, 30.)
2. The Islamic military forced Egyptians to speak Arabic instead of their native Coptic. People who refused could have their tongues cut out. The details are in a book titled *The History of the Church in Egypt* by Iris al Massri (book published in Cairo).
3. Armstrong, *Islam: A Short History*, 10.
4. *Approaching the Qu'ran*, trans. Michael Sells (Ashland, OR: White Cloud Press, 1999).

CHAPTER 10: DOES MY MUSLIM NEIGHBOR BELIEVE IN JIHAD?

1. A popular new book, *Militant Islam Reaches America*, uses the term *moderate Muslim* in reference to a Muslim who is not an "Islamicist." [Daniel Pipes, *Militant Islam Reaches America* (New York: Norton, 2002), 143.]
2. Andrea Stone, "Many in Islamic world doubt Arabs behind 9/11," *USA Today* (February 27, 2002).
3. Michael Schaffer, "The Claims of the Deniers," *U.S. News and World Report* (September 16, 2002): 48.
4. "Terror, Lies and Videotape," Washington, May 15, 2002, from cbsnews.com at www.cbsnews.com/stories/2002/05/14/attack/main509059.shtml.

CHAPTER 11: SETTING THE STAGE

1. Dr. Ti-Nagar, *The Life of the Prophet* (Cairo, Egypt). The author of this book was one of my teachers at Al-Azhar University. He later became president of the university.
2. Dr. A. Shalaby, *Encyclopedia of Islamic History* (Cairo,

Egypt: Dar al-Nahadah). See also Surah 2:113.

3. Abu Musa Al Hariri, *Priest and Prophet* (Beirut, Lebanon).

CHAPTER 12: THE QURAN'S NICE WORDS ABOUT JEWS

1. *The Noble Quran* claims that this verse also mentions obedience to the Quran, but this interpretation is not evident in Arabic.

CHAPTER 13: JEWS RESIST MUHAMMAD'S CLAIMS TO THEIR GOD AND THEIR SCRIPTURES

1. This chart was created through a content analysis of the entire Quran. The analysis was conducted by a graduate of the University of Florida with a master's degree in mass communication. First, the researcher read the Quran, taking notes on the places where biblical stories occurred. Then the Quran was reviewed again, and the list was created. The guidelines for a story to be included in the list were:
   - The story must have an overall similarity to the Bible story. (An asterisk was added to indicate where most of the story matched the Bible version, but some new material was also added.)
   - It must be a story of two or more sentences, not just a mention of a biblical character. (Therefore, references to the "religion of Abraham," for example, would not be included.)
   - This list does not include references to biblical teaching, such as discussion of Judgment Day, Satan, sin, etc.

   The researcher described the stories using terms that would be familiar to Christian readers, even if that term is not in the Quran; for example, she would say "Noah and the ark" rather than "Noah and the ship."

2. Jews were not the first to target Muhammad. The idol worshipers in Mecca had already tried to kill him.

3. Ibn Husham, *The Biography of the Prophet,* vol. 2 (Cairo, Egypt: Al-Maktabah As-Salafiya), 308–309.

CHAPTER 14: THE QURAN CANCELS THE KIND WORDS ABOUT THE JEWS

1. This teaching is not only in the Quran. It is also in Quranic commentaries, the books that discuss the prophet of Islam and the books of Islamic history.

CHAPTER 15: EXPANDING THE CASE AGAINST THE JEWS

1. The Covenant of Hamas—Main Points, retrieved from Internet on December 12, 2002 at www.hraic.org/ the_covenant_of_hamas.html.

CHAPTER 16: MUHAMMAD PREPARES TO DRIVE THE JEWS OUT OF ARABIA

1. Sayyid Qutb, *In the Shadow of the Quran,* a Quranic commentary (Cairo, Egypt and Beirut, Lebanon: Dar el-Shorouk International).

CHAPTER 17: THE ARABIAN HOLOCAUST

1. I have not included the story of the Qaynuqa tribe, which was expelled from Medina in 624. Their story is similar to what happened to the Nadir.
2. Some books say that Muhammad attacked the Nadir tribe because they collaborated with the idol worshipers of Mecca in the Battle of Uhud during this same year. The Jews might have helped the Meccans a little bit, but there is not much evidence to support this in Islamic history.
3. Ibn Kathir, the historian scholar.
4. *A Historical Atlas of the Jewish People,* ed. by Eli Barnavi (New York: Schocken Books, 1992), 74.
5. Ibn Husham, vol. 2, 144.
6. Ibn Ishaq, Islamic historian and scholar.
7. Ibn Husham, vol. 2, 146.
8. Al-Tabari, *The King and the Prophets.*
9. Ibn Husham, vol. 2, 193.

10. Ibid., 201.
11. Ibid.
12. Ibid., 205.
13. Ibid., 299.
14. Ibid., 307.
15. Ibid., 326.
16. Ibn Kathir, *The Beginning and the End.*
17. Armstrong, *Islam: A Short History,* 21.
18. Al-Bukhari.
19. The specific number of seventy virgins is mentioned in hadith, not in the Quran.
20. Ibn-Husham, vol. 2, 316.

CHAPTER 18: MUSLIMS CONTINUE MUHAMMAD'S LEGACY

1. This list was compiled from the following sources: Dr. Kasim Abdo, *People of the Book in Egypt During the Middle Ages* (Cairo, Egypt: Dar-al-Maerif, 1977), 26–27; Al-Tabori, *The History of the Kings and the Prophets* (Cairo, Egypt: Dar-al-Maerif); Ibn-Kathir, *The Beginning and the End* (Cairo, Egypt: Al-Maktaba As-Salafiya).
2. Mitchell Bard, "The Treatment of Jews in Arab/Islamic Countries." Retrieved from the Internet at Jewish Virtual Library at www.us-israel.org, 2002.
3. Ibid.
4. For more details, see Bard, "The Treatment of Jews in Arab/Islamic Countries."
5. Abdo, *People of the Book in Egypt During the Middle Ages,* 56.
6. *A Historical Atlas of the Jewish People,* 81.
7. Ibid., 83.
8. Ibid., 93.
9. Muslims are very aware that the war was started by the Christian church of the West, specifically the Roman Catholic Church, not the Orthodox churches of Eastern Europe, Russia and the Middle East.
10. Dr. Mohammed Ashoor, *Europe in the Dark Ages* (Dar al-Nahadah). This author was one of my professors at Al-Azhar

University. This is the most respected book on this topic in Islamic education.

11. You can read the complete text of Osama bin Laden's essay in Appendix B.

CHAPTER 20: A CALL TO WAR FOR ISLAM

1. Dr. A. Shinauwi, *Uthman Dynasty: Islamic State.* This is a book I studied during the third year of my bachelor degree. It is the most respected modern Islamic history book. All Islamic universities around the world use this book. I also used it as a textbook when I was a teacher.

2. *Islamic world* and *Arabic world* refer to two different sets of nations. The Islamic world means the countries where the majority of the people practice Islam. This includes more than fifty-five countries around the world. The Arabic world refers to those countries where Islam is the majority religion *and* Arabic is the first language. The Arabic world includes twenty-two countries in the Middle East and North Africa.

3. They liked to use the slogan, "Islam is the solution." They used this slogan the way Christians use the saying, "Jesus is the answer."

4. The only pure Islamic states in modern times are Iran, Sudan and the former government of Afghanistan. Saddam Hussein of Iraq and Muammar Qaddafi of Libya are Muslim dictators, but they are not running their countries as pure Islamic states. Fanatic Muslims would love to kill them.

5. Hussein has held on to his attitude against Israel. In the 1990s, he threatened to burn Israel to the ground. ("How Saddam Happened," *Newsweek* [September 23, 2002]: 22–37.

CHAPTER 21: THE FRONT LINES: PALESTINIANS VS. ISRAEL

1. Information Division, Israel Foreign Ministry: www.israel-mfa.gov.il. The Covenant of the Islamic Resistance Movement (also known as Hamas) was issued on August 18, 1988. Also, The Covenant of Hamas—Main Points, retrieved from Internet on December 12. 2002 at www.hraic.org/

the_covenant_of_hamas.html.

2. Abdullah Alnafisy, *No to Normalization With Israel*, 2nd edition (Michigan: The Islamic Assembly of North America, 2000).

3. There are three most holy sites in Islam. The first is the al-Kaaba in Mecca, Saudi Arabia; the second is the Mosque of the Prophet in Medina, Saudi Arabia, where Muhammad is buried. Both of these places are off limits to non-Muslims. That means a Jew or Christian is not allowed to lay eyes on the great black rock (the Kaaba) or to set foot inside the prophet's mosque.

4. If you would like to read the complete text of bin Laden's *fatwa*, see Appendix B. Retrieved from Internet at www.fas.org/irp/world/para/does/980223-fatwa.htm.

5. A detailed account of the Jewish attempts to take over the Dome of the Rock, with more than fifty incidents since the 1960s, is given in *The Jews' Secret Activity* by Khalil abd al-Karim (Beirut, Lebanon: Sinai Publishing, 1991).

6. Article by Oleg Artyukov in *Pravda*, a Russian newspaper, translated by Maria Gousseva. Obtained on the Internet.

7. Alnafisy, *No to Normalization With Israel*.

8. Ibid., 6–35.

9. The Covenant of Hamas—Main Points, retrieved from Internet on December 12, 2002 at www.hraic.org/the_covenant_of_hamas.html.

10. Ibid.

11. Article by Arnold Beichman, a Hoover Institute Research Fellow, who is a columnist for the Washington Times. Retrieved from Internet at www.washtimes.com/commentary/beichman.htm.

12. Alnafisy, *No to Normalization with Israel*, 6–35.

13. The CBN program was called "The Jihad Trail."

14. BBC news article titled "Female bomber's mother speaks out," retrieved from Internet at news.bbc.co.uk on January 30, 2002.

Chapter 22: Muslims Believe Jews Hate Them

1. "Israeli Haughtiness, and How It Will End: A Noted Islamist

Writer Predicts the End of Israel From the Quran."
Originally printed in *Al-Ahram International*, May 17, 1997,
retrieved from the web site www.ahram.org. Translation
from Arabic by Mounir Bishay. *Al-Ahram* is Egypt's largest
Arabic newspaper, printed in English and Arabic and distrib-
uted all over the world.

2. *Threatening and Challenging*, first edition (Riad City, Saudi
Arabia: 2000).

CHAPTER 25: THE STRUGGLES OF THE MIDDLE EASTERN CHURCH

1. Rajeb Al Banah, *Interviews With Pope Shenuda* (Cairo,
Egypt: Dar-Al-Maarif, 1997), 242–265.
2. Ibid.
3. Ibid.
4. Ikram Lamae, *Is There Any Relation Between the Second
Coming of Jesus Christ and the Return of the Jews to the
Promised Land?* (Cairo, Egypt: Dar Al-Sakafah, 1990), 14.
5. Al Banah, *Interviews With Pope Shenuda*.

APPENDIX A: ABRAHAM AND ISHMAEL: WHO TELLS THE REAL STORY?

1. Millions of lambs are sacrificed during the month of *hajj*.
Muslim authorities in Saudi Arabia freeze the lambs and dis-
tribute them to poor people in many Islamic countries.
2. From this statement, we should assume that Ishmael was
two years old or less because Islam says a child should be
nursed for two years, but not longer.
3. Summarized and paraphrased from Al-Bukhari.
4. The Arabic word translated as *forbearing* means, "One who
is not easily provoked." This description is in great contrast
to the biblical description of Ishmael: "He will be a wild
donkey of a man; his hand will be against everyone and
everyone's hand against him, and he will live in hostility
toward all his brothers" (Gen. 16:12).
5. Syed Muhammad Hussain Shamsi, *The Prophets of Islam*

(Englewood, NJ: Alhuda Foundation, 1994).
6. Al-Bukhari, vol 4, No. 583.

APPENDIX B: OSAMA BIN LADEN:
JIHAD AGAINST JEWS AND CRUSADERS

1. The text of this statement was found on the Internet at www.fas.org/irp/world/para/docs/980223-fatwa.htm. It was published in the Arabic Newspaper *al-Quds al-Arabi* (London, U.K.) on 23 February 1998 on page 3. It is also a part of the Middle East and Islamic Studies Collection at Cornell University Library.
2. Ibid.

APPENDIX C: THE BIBLICAL PROPHECIES
ISLAM CLAIMS FOR MUHAMMAD

1. Surah 5:13 speaks specifically about the Jews. Surah 5:14 makes a similar statement about Christians.
2. See the footnote to Surah 7:157 in *The Noble Quran.*
3. For the sake of space, I did not quote the entire passage cited by the Muslim scholars, which was Isaiah 42:1–13.

OTHER BOOKS BY THE AUTHOR

Islam and Terrorism (Charisma House, 2002)—What the Quran really teaches about Christianity, violence and the goals of the Islamic jihad

For information about having Dr. Mark Gabriel speak at your church, conference or school, contact:

Hope for the Nations
Mark A. Gabriel
P. O. Box 181974
Casselberry, FL 32718-1974